The present study is a product of the Development Centre's research programme on "Food for All": The Capacity of Developing Countries to Meet their Food Requirements". This programme was initiated as part of the Centre's research programme on Interdependence and Development. It has involved the collaboration of researchers and institutions in developing countries and OECD Member countries in varying degrees at different stages of its implementation.

Also available

THE FOOD SITUATION AND POLICIES IN THE REPUBLIC OF KOREA by Dong-Hi Kim and Yong-Jae Joo «Document» Series (February 1983)
(41 82 03 1) ISBN 92-64-12382-2   116 pages
                                                            £4.70   US$9.50   F47.00

SATISFACTION OF FOOD REQUIREMENTS IN MALI TO 2000 A.D. by Jacqueline Mondot-Bernard and Michel Labonne (September 1982)
(41 82 01 1) ISBN 92-64-12300-8   214 pages
                                                            £6.80   US$15.00   F68.00

FOOD AID FOR DEVELOPMENT by Hartmut Schneider (March 1979)
(41 78 06 1) ISBN 92-64-11862-4   132 pages
                                                            £3.30   US$6.75   F27.00

PLANNING FOR GROWING POPULATIONS edited by Robert Cassen and Margaret Wolfson with an Introduction by Göran Ohlin (February 1979)
(41 78 03 1) ISBN 92-64-11830-6   228 pages
                                                            £5.60   US$11.50   F46.00

TABLE OF CONTENTS

Chapter III
IMPORTS AND THE DOMESTIC FOOD CHAIN

Chapter IV
DOMESTIC STRUCTURAL CHANGE AND POLICY OPTIONS

Chapter V
OUTLOOK

LIST OF TABLES

Acknowledgements

This report, while drawing on the literature at large, also relies (and sometimes heavily so) on papers prepared in the context of the Development Centre's research programme on Food for All: The Capacity of Developing Countries to Meet Their Food Requirements. While these papers are not being published, credit should be given to their authors. Thus a general paper largely used for the first chapter has been contributed by Brian van Arkadie. Country papers have been prepared by Slimane Bedrani on Algeria, by Thomas Eponou on the Ivory Coast, and by Allan Bollard on the South Pacific Islands (in addition to the report on Korea by Dong Hi-Kim and Yong Jae Joo which has been published separately).

Duncan Miller, who was in charge of this project at its inception, contributed a paper on food insecurity and Winifred Weekes-Vagliani provided a review of socio-cultural factors and government policies in Mexico, Peru and the Ivory Coast. Jacqueline Mondot-Bernard reported on food consumption and nutrition in Sahelian countries and Jane Ramin wrote on agricultural input markets in developing countries.

Acknowledgements are also due to a large number of people who took part in discussions and contributed ideas at various stages of the project. While they are too numerous to be all named here, special thanks are due to Professor Jacques Bourrinet, University of Aix-Marseille III and to Professor John S. Marsh, University of Aberdeen, as well as to our colleagues in the OECD Directorates for Agriculture and Development Co-operation for commenting on earlier versions of this report.

Over the last decade, the food and agriculture sector has gained pro-
minence in both the theory and the practice of development. In this study,
emphasis is placed on the links between national food sytems and international
trade. The analysis seeks to combine different perspectives and to strike a
balance between opposing schools of thought, one emphasizing the distortions
which exposure to the world economy may impose on the domestic food systems of
developing countries, and the other concentrating on the potential gains from
a high degree of integration of developing contries' agriculture in the world
economy through foreign trade. The study draws special attention to the
implications of alternative policies for different groups of producers and
consumers.

This report is aimed primarily at those who, at different levels, are
involved in decision-making with regard to food policies of developing countries. But given the fundamental character of the need for food and also the
central place of agriculture in the economic structure and in the development
strategy of most poor countries, the report should also be of interest to the
larger community of those concerned with general development policies.

The context of change in which the food policies of developing
countries are examined in this report refers to both the national and international levels. Altered patterns of international trade in food and
agricultural commodities have made certain countries very vulnerable to fluctuations and even, in some cases, unable to meet their regular food requirements. Consequently, food security has become a major international concern.
National governments are preoccupied with domestic food production, often
setting targets of increased self-sufficiency. Policies to meet such targets
are not always easy to design and implement, in particular because of their
implications for efficiency, income distribution and domestic structural
change.

The research was based on the hypothesis that food problems should be
seen in the context of a "food system" which is itself linked to the economic
structure of a country and is thus subject to both internal and external
forces to varying degrees. The first chapter outlines major economic propositions and issues in a general way. It recalls fundamental economic relations
which set the framework for any food system and which sometimes seem to be
ignored in the discussion of more specific food issues.

The chapters which follow examine the role in the food system of agricultural exports and imports, and of domestic structural change, reflecting
the perspective of interdependence taken in this report. Throughout, emphasis
has been placed on the need for disaggregation and, more specifically, on the
need to identify the mechanisms which affect various groups of producers and
consumers differently. Wherever appropriate and possible, general hypotheses

of a bias in development policies against food production for domestic consumption, against small producers and in favour of urban areas have been examined, and an effort has been made to identify policies which would mitigate distortions and reduce insecurity at minimal cost.

The final chapter, on the outlook for the future, deals with questions of needs and resource use which are referred to in various ways throughout the text but which were considered sufficiently important to deserve special attention. In the same spirit, the last section underlines the need for scope for coherent policy choices and reviews the role of external assistance.

Food issues are dealt with in many specialised fora, such as the Food and Agricultural Organisation, the World Food Council and the World Food Programme, to name only a few from within the United Nations family. While their reports have been used, together with many others, no attempt has been made here to refer to their important and wide-ranging activities in any systematic way. In particular, the issue of food security has been dealt with more implicitly than explicitly and not at all in terms of the technical discussion underway elsewhere (e.g. the Committee on Food Security at FAO). The relevant specialised organisations, together with smaller research-oriented institutes, are listed and briefly described in a Directory of Food Policy Institutes which was prepared as a by-product of the research undertaken at the Development Centre.

Just Faaland
President
OECD Development Centre
January 1984

Chapter I

FOOD IN THE OVERALL ECONOMIC STRUCTURE: SOME BASIC PROPOSITIONS AND ISSUES (1)

1. FOOD PRODUCTION: THE POLITICAL AND INSTITUTIONAL DETERMINANTS

As food is one of the most basic human needs, it might be thought unnecessary to discuss its function in relation to other parts of the economic
and social system. Food supply must surely be the first priority of economic
activity. In the first instance, other economic objectives should properly be
subservient; indeed, other economic activity can only exist if the need for
food is met first.

While that perception is morally and/or politically correct and justi-
fies the great emphasis on food issues in development programming and research, a little thought will indicate why the food issue must nevertheless be
examined in the context of the broader range of economic activities.

The first, and most obvious, point is that food supply does not necessarily imply food production. Indeed, in certain respects there may be an
inverse relationship between food self-sufficiency within a given economic
unit and security of food supplies. It is by no means always the case that
those involved in food production have privileged access to food; malnutrition and famine are, if anything, more rural than urban phenomena.

Specialisation is often associated with high productivity and flexibility. In extreme cases (e.g. Singapore) food supply will necessarily
involve trade. In other cases, even if imports are not an absolute necessity,
the procurement of food may still be more effectively secured through concentration on non-food production. Historically, this has occurred not only when
economies have become industrial exporters but also when agricultural capacity
has been shifted to non-food exports (e.g. colonial Ceylon, where the development of the tea industry was associated with the growth of cheap food
imports). Food has to be placed in the larger economic context in order to
determine to what extent food supply is most effectively secured through food
production.

Secondly, even if food supply should, in a moral/political sense, be of
the highest priority, the factors which determine food policy are likely to
include other requirements of the economic system. Thus, when industrialisation represents another priority, the effects of food prices on urban wages

12

and the profitability of industry may be critical determinants of food policy.

Thirdly, because food is such a basic need, its control may at times be an extremely important element of political power and strategy. Soviet collectivisation, for example, was primarily a political act. In Britain, the repeal of the Corn Laws in 1846, in response to the emerging needs of an industrialising economy, represented a shift in the locus of political influence.

Food supply may become a crucial factor in political struggle not only within the nation but also in the balance of power among countries. Of course, difficulty in financing food imports is just one facet of a general balance-of-payments problem, but it assumes particular importance because of the non-postponable nature of food import requirements.

When food supply is discussed in the context of the economic and political relations between sectors, the nature of the categories used must be clarified in order to avoid ambiguity. The food-producing sector (and the agricultural sector in general) is often distinguished from other sectors less by the inherent attributes of its product than by the form of organisation of production. Thus "food" may be seen as the product of the "traditional" sector or of the "peasantry", or of a "pre-capitalist feudal system". Consequently, the relationship between different commodities in the market can be seen as a reflection of relations between differing modes of production. While such a presentation may be used in abstract discussion, the wide variations in economic organisation of food production in most developing countries renders the assumption of a homogeneous "sector" suspect at the outset.

In a fully industrialised society, the nature of the "food" question changes because the form of organisation of agriculture (e.g. technology, capital intensity, corporate form) tends to resemble that of industry. Agriculture will, of course, still have identifiable interests, just like the steel industry or the automobile industry, but, qualitatively, it can no longer be so readily identified as a distinct form of economic organisation.

Nevertheless, even when agriculture acquires some of the technical characteristics of industry (e.g. in the use of power and of manufactured inputs), it may retain distinguishing characteristics with respect to its social organisation (e.g. the persistence of the family farm). Moreover, much agricultural activity remains dependent on climatic conditions with resulting uncertainties.

The intrusion of modern agro-business into a developing economy has to be treated with some analytical care. Is it to be seen as a revival of plantation agriculture, with its dependence on assured supplies of low-cost labour, or is it a facet of the expansion of the "modern", "industrial" sector, presenting similar problems of assessment as multinational investment in industry?

In so far as commodity trade between agriculture and the non-agricultural sectors of the economy involves an exchange between different groups in society, the reasons for apparent failures in food production policy should be sought not only at the technical or intellectual level. Inadequacies in food policy are also likely to result from various economic pressures which influence the choice of policy objectives and from the changing political balance within the society. For example, the terms of trade faced by agriculture may be, either implicitly or explicitly, a key matter of contention between major political groups.

As an additional introductory observation, the simple and now generally accepted economic point should be made that a necessary prerequisite to food consumption is not only food availability or supply but also effective demand. Public intervention to procure food for those in need may complement the demand expressed directly at the market. Furthermore, if it lowers the food price, expansion in food supply will expand access to food. Food production and consumption patterns are thus inevitably connected with income distribution.

In analysing the circumstances in which food deficiency occurs, it is therefore important to distinguish the cases where deficiencies can be resolved by a technical "fix" on the supply side from cases where the existing pattern of income distribution prevents segments of the population from purchasing adequate food at or around existing price levels.

However, while income determines effective demand for, and access to, food supplies, the pattern of food production is, in turn, an important determinant of income distribution. Thus it is possible not only that increases in agricultural productivity may fail to increase food consumption, but that if such increases have regressive effects on income distribution, they could be associated with a decline in food consumption at the lower income levels (and even a fall in total food consumption). Although no generalisation can be made, this may be more than a formal logical possibility; commentators have suggested a number of historical instances in which dramatic increases in agricultural productivity have been associated with rural pauperisation.

Thus, while the satisfaction of food requirements at world level can be seen as primarily a matter of ensuring adequate food output, access by a particular individual, group or community to food is a function of its economic and political power rather than its ability to grow food. The great cities of the industrial world enjoy diverse and secure food supplies, without producing food, precisely because of their location in a large economic and political structure. Deficiency or insecurity of food supply always reflects a more general economic and political vulnerability. Expanded food production may, in some circumstances, contribute to a reduction in that vulnerability, but is neither a necessary nor sufficient condition for the achievement of that end in all cases.

2. INTER-SECTORAL RELATIONS IN A CLOSED ECONOMY

As a first step in an analysis of the role of food in the economy, it may be useful to consider some basic propositions about inter-sectoral relationships in a simple closed economy.

In the earlier stages of historical development, surplus food production over and above the subsistence needs of the labour required for its production is a necessary condition for the development of non-agricultural activity. The potential to produce such a surplus exists in a subsistence economy when labour is not fully utilised (as described, for example, by W. Arthur Lewis), i.e. when some labour can be withdrawn from food production without there necessarily being a loss of input and the remaining labour is capable of producing food in excess of its own subsistence needs. However, to feed the non-agricultural labour force, food must be transferred through trade, tribute, tax or rent.

Thus the existence of towns presupposes the possibility of producing an agricultural surplus. However, the explicit realisation of the agricultural surplus requires the appearance of a demand for food from outside the subsistence system.

The sequence can be envisaged as follows: growth outside the subsistence sector occurs, the subsistence frees labour and supplies the food for its sustenance. In addition to absorbing labour, this growth may also provide the impetus for increases in agricultural output. The "unlimited supply" (i.e. zero marginal product) of labour in subsistence agriculture is not necessarily the result of zero marginal physical product. It may equally be a measure of the limited value of additional food production when there is no demand from outside the subsistence system. Thus agricultural improvement beyond the satisfaction of subsistence needs presupposes the growth of non-agricultural activities.

Food production and non-agricultural activity will be linked through the trade of commodities, by which food is exchanged for goods and services, through the movement of labour from agriculture, and through the transfer of rents and taxes. Moreover, because of the importance of food in the budgets of workers at low income levels, food prices are an important determinant of the real wage: the higher the level of food prices, the higher the non-agricultural wage necessary to meet workers' living requirements and the greater the pressure on the profit share in the non-agricultural sector. It is therefore not only the consumer who is interested in low food prices but also the employer.

In principle, there are three mechanisms whereby food procurement can be expanded to meet non-agricultural needs while allowing part of the product of the non-agricultural sector to be diverted to non-agricultural accumulation:

a) agriculture can be "squeezed", either by a deterioration in terms of trade, so that an increasing agricultural effort is required to acquire a given quantum of non-agricultural goods, or by more direct appropriation of the agricultural product, e.g. through taxation;

b) increases in agricultural productivity may induce a shift in the terms of trade against agriculture, so that a given quantum of non-agricultural products is exchanged for an increasing amount of food, although the agricultural sector receives a constant return in terms of non-agricultural goods for its supply of effort. That is, the benefits of agricultural progress are reaped through the market by the non-agricultural sector;

c) increase in non-agricultural output may allow more non-agricultural products to be allocated for food procurement without any decline in the rate of non-agricultural profit (i.e. a given proportion of the non-agricultural workforce produces a greater quantity of output).

The benefits of non-agricultural productivity growth are shared by the agriculturalist through a shift in the terms of trade in favour of agriculture.

In the light of these possibilities, a virtuous development sequence might be expected to take something like the following path:

i)   initially, the existence of surplus labour in the agricultural sector creates the possibility for non-agricultural growth; as labour is withdrawn from agriculture, the food that would have been consumed within the sector can be transferred without a consumption loss to those remaining (although on average they may have to work harder -- hence the need for an incentive or compulsion to transfer surplus food). The stimulus of trade possibilities with the non-agricultural sector may lead to the realisation of an additional food surplus, not previously produced because of a lack of demand;

ii) as the non-agricultural sector grows, improved productivity in agriculture allows the required increase in food procurement on terms which permit a high rate of non-agricultural accumulation;

iii) as the economy moves towards maturity, increases in non-agricultural productivity could make possible a shift in the terms of trade in favour of agriculture, so that the agricultural sector benefits from the fruits of technical progress in the non-agricultural sector.

While this outline may be useful for the understanding of macro-economic processes, there are dangers in over-simplification. The image which emerges is that of a pool of under-employed rural labour which is both ready and willing to shift to other economic activities and is able to do so without entailing losses in rural production.

However, the withdrawal of labour can often have negative effects on production. An apparent surplus of labour can conceal the existence of labour constraints on output (e.g. seasonal scarcities; the use of labour for certain non-recurrent tasks, such as land-clearing and terracing). This is particularly likely to be the case if the dynamic impact of population pressure on agricultural innovation is taken into account, that is, if rural de-population reduces pressures within rural society for improvements in productivity.

Often, moreover, the proletarianisation of "surplus" labour has not been as spontaneous as this image implies but has involved systematic acts of policy, including coercion, to shift labour into new lines of activity. There are historical examples in which policies depressing productivity levels in the agricultural sector have been used to lower the opportunity cost of labour (e.g. in colonial Africa, protecting settlers from competition from small-holder farming in the labour market).

An analysis of alternative forms of organisation in the "traditional" rural economy could carry the analysis forward. The discussion in the previous paragraphs draws on African experience of a somewhat socially undifferentiated rural society. This is only one of a number of relevant models of rural economic organisation, based on different systems of land tenure and organisation of labour.

In the case of the family small-holding, the extraction of a surplus from the agriculture sector will depend very much on conditions in the commodity market (e.g. the marketing of agricultural products, and the rural/urban terms of trade). In a landlord/tenant system, the imposition of rents might provide the basis for surplus extraction. In plantation agriculture labour market conditions are likely to influence profitability, which in turn might provide the basis for surplus extraction.

Returning to the virtuous sequence described above, as a rough model of a possible process of development, such a process may be interrupted by faltering productivity growth in either agriculture or non-agriculture. If there is a setback in agricultural production, then the non-agricultural sector may have to allocate a higher proportion of its output to ensure required food procurement, thus undermining the pace of its own expansion. Alternatively, any decline in non-agricultural output will make it more difficult for this sector to release the goods it needs to trade for food.

To deal with difficulties arising from productive failures in either the agricultural or non-agricultural sectors, two distinct paths can be pursued (2). Either the pace of non-agricultural growth can be reduced, diverting resources from non-agricultural accumulation to the agricultural sector, with the hope that the incentives thus provided plus the availability of resources will spur productivity growth in agriculture and allow subsequent resumption of the pace of non-agricultural accumulation. That is, the initial burden of faltering productivity growth is borne by a reduction in the non-agricultural accumulation effort. Or, the agricultural sector can be squeezed to provide the required food without any reduction in non-agricultural accumulation. In this case, pressure on the agricultural sector is subsequently eased when the flow of non-agricultural commodities makes it possible to increase the availability of food to the agricultural sector. The initial burden is then borne by the agricultural sector.

The economic consequences of adopting one course or the other will depend on the potential supply responses in the two sectors.

It is not suggested that policy options are thought out explicitly along the lines implied by the simple schema above. Food price policies, for example, are likely to respond to short-term political pressures rather than a grand view of economic strategy.

The indirect effects of policies mounted for quite other purposes (e.g. industrialisation policies) may be as important for the real income of food producers as the effects of those policy instruments explicitly utilised to implement food policies. Nevertheless, the basic relationships outlined determine possible constraints on a wide range of economic policies; they also influence more obvious phenomena in day-to-day politics.

3. FOOD IN THE OPEN ECONOMY

Some of the possible modifications in inter-sectoral relations result-ing from the development of economic links with the international economy are examined briefly in the following paragraphs. The intention is to simplify a potentially high complex set of inter-relationships. The main concern is with the effects of trade, although some reference is made to effects of investment and labour migration.

The discussion provides a stylised version of alternative economic structures, drawing conclusions about some of the implications of particular structural characteristics for food policy; at this stage it falls short of providing either a comprehensive typology or fully elaborated economic models.

The structural characteristics relate to different forms of:

a) competition on the supply side between export production and food production;

b) competition between domestic and imported food; and

c) some indirect effects of the changing economic environment on subsistence food systems.

Some of the principal characteristics of the experience of a number of developing countries are reflected in a scenario whereby initial integration into the international economy through the export of cash crops was followed by a period of industrialisation through import substitution.

In such a sequence, international trade modifies inter-sectoral relationships as follows:

i) both the agricultural and the non-agricultural sectors utilise imported commodities;

ii) the agricultural sector can become a significant source of foreign exchange earnings through the export of either food or non-food agricultural products;

iii) exports thus become competitive with food production for domestic use;

iv) access of the non-agricultural sector to imported goods will depend on generation by the agricultural sector of surplus foreign exchange above its own requirements and transfer of this surplus to the non-agricultural sector;

v) in the early stages of primary commodity production, the transfer of surplus foreign exchange to the non-agricultural sector can be through such mechanisms as:

a) the agricultural sector supplies export goods to the world market and food to the non-agricultural sector;

b) the non-agricultural sector supplies import-substitute industrial goods to the agricultural sector;

c) the international economy supplies industrial goods (and in particular capital and intermediate goods) to both non-agricultural and agricultural sectors.

In this situation, accumulation in the non-agricultural sector is potentially constrained either by the supply of food from the agricultural sector or by the supply of foreign exchange, also derived from the output of the agricultural sector.

The real income which the agricultural sector derives from its production will depend on:

a) international prices (i.e. external terms of trade);

b) the domestic price level for goods supplied by the non-agricultural sector (and for food supplied to the non-agricultural sector); and

c) the transfer of surplus through non-trade mechanisms (taxes, etc.).

The agricultural sector may therefore find itself under pressure due to deterioration in the international terms of trade, inefficiency in the recurrent production activities of the non-agricultural sector, or the demands of the non-agricultural sector for real resources for capital accumulation.

The negative impact of policy on food production is not likely to result from explicit intentions, such as the promotion of cheap food imports or a calculated neglect of agricultural investment. Rather, problems are likely to emerge as a result of the indirect effects of other policies and short-term response to economic difficulties. It is not untypical for planning documents and government statements to place great emphasis on food production, although in the event the impact of policies adopted to push the economy in a quite different direction.

Thus industrial protection measures associated with import substitution shift the terms of trade against agriculture. If, partly as a result of this, there is a deterioration in export performance and heightened balance-of-payments difficulties, a likely response will be special measures to boost the farm price of export crops, further depressing the relative profitability of food crop production.

One likely outcome of this sequence is a decline in the domestic food supply which leads to an increase in food imports and a worsening of the external payments crisis. In response, there is likely to be a rhetorical commitment by the public authorities to the expansion of food output and even some diversion of public resources to support food production. However, this is likely to result in increased food output only if real resources are released from other uses to provide farmers with a higher return for their production, i.e. if there is a real shift in the terms of trade in favour of food production.

The short-term policy dilemma is very clear in cases where the major export crop is also a staple food, so that the same production process supplies both the export and the domestic food markets. Argentina and Thailand are examples of such a structure. It is possible to shift food output quite directly from domestic markets to export markets, and vice versa. One possible policy instrument to achieve this is adjustment in the foreign exchange rate. Devaluation shifts food into export trade, increasing the availability of foreign exchange, but at the same time reducing non-agricultural real wages. If reductions in real wages are not accepted, either inflation wipes out the effect of the devaluation, or non-agricultural profits are squeezed and food supplies to the non-agricultural sector restored but at a higher cost to the non-agricultural sector (whose potential rate of growth is consequently reduced).

Where agriculture has traditionally produced food for export, a ready flexibility can be expected between producing for the home and export markets. Where there is little experience of food exporting, a particular policy problem arises. If the agricultural system is geared to producing food for subsistence and purely local markets, a small proportion of output being purchased for current urban use or stocked for future use, it may be possible to provide a guaranteed price at -- or even somewhat above -- the import parity price. When self-sufficiency is achieved, there is a need to dispose of surplus food production over and above domestic needs. Commercial transport and storage inadequacies are likely to mean a very large gap between import and export price parities, resulting in heavy financial costs in the event of the need to export. Moreover, where the farmer supplies the commercial market only after meeting subsistence and local market needs, deliveries are likely to fluctuate much more widely than total production. The farmer will meet his own needs first and sell only his surplus to the market, so that commercial sales bear the full brunt of output fluctuation. In such a situation, the maintenance of a price policy which ensures average year-to-year food produc- tion levels to satisfy the national market will be quite a tricky exercise.

Where agricultural exports are not food staples and substitution of food and export production is not direct, the short-term cross-elasticity of supply may be quite low, if, for example, substitution requires redirection of land use and of labour in the production process over one or more seasons.

At the extreme, the development of non-food export agriculture may involve a degree of specialisation in production which eliminates short-term flexibility. Thus plantation production of tree crops may involve a commit- ment of capital and land which is not readily adaptable to food production in the short-term. This is not merely the result of agronomic characteristics. Once capital is sunk into tree crops, maintenance of the capacity will be economically justified in the short term as long as revenues cover recurrent costs. Institutional commitment (e.g. under the managing agency system) to a particular line of production may also limit flexibility.

Under conditions of very limited short-term flexibility, the policy problem is not so much the manipulation of policy instruments to achieve short-term adjustments between production for the home and the export markets (depending on the stringency of the external resource or food supply con- straints) as the impact of policies on the longer-term balance in the growth of two activities, food and export crop production, which might in some institutional situations be viewed as distinct "industries" or even "sectors".

Thus much commentary on African colonial (and post-colonial) agriculture has noted the longer-term consequences of concentrating agricultural research, extension and infrastructural development on the needs of export agriculture, be it plantation or smallholder agriculture, to the detriment of food crop development.

Insofar as that was (or is) the case, it should be noted that this did not result merely from official whims, or economic error. The fundamental basis of economic growth was the mobilisation of surplus labour for export production, to provide the fiscal and material bases of the colonial (and post-colonial) state. Surplus labour, as was noted above, essentially means available manpower plus food. In the case of smallholder production, it can be argued that a necessary (if unstated) assumption of colonial agriculture in a number of African countries was that "subsistence" production would meet labour force food needs without requiring additional resources, and that, particularly in smallholder export crop systems, food production could be left to look after itself. This is not to say, however, that in the face of neglect subsistence food production remained unchanged in a "traditional" production system that persisted alongside the cash-crop production system. Concurrently with the extension of cash-cropping, equally profound changes in food crop production took place, resulting from both an informal process of technical diffusion and the economic consequences of cash-crop specialisation.

In plantation agriculture, the system more typically depended on a migratory labour force whose own connection with the land had been severed (or at least attenuated by distance). In such cases, feeding the labour force was a critical problem. While this could be done through subsistence production (e.g. "squatters" on European-owned farms in Kenya), large-scale agriculture could only guarantee its access to cheap labour if access by the labour force to its own land were limited. It is not surprising, therefore, that plantation agriculture had to turn to labour which migrated over long distances rather than to the local peasantry (e.g. Indian labour in Ceylon and Fiji).

In this situation, insofar as the labour force migrated without their families, "subsistence" production contributed to the reproduction of the labour force, through the sustenance of the family at home. However, it should be noted that the withdrawal of an active element from the rural labour force could lead to deterioration in the subsistence agricultural system.

The problem of feeding the plantation labour force itself was in some cases handled through food imports. Perhaps the most classic case was that of colonial Ceylon, where the growth of the tea industry in the decades before the World War I was combined with the expansion of the Indian migrant labour force and a parallel growth in food imports (cheap rice from Burma and Thailand). How far is plantation export agriculture typically associated with dependence on food imports? (There are a number of unanswered questions regarding, for example, the poor performance of local food production throughout much of the Caribbean -- and the resulting dependence on food imports.) Plantation agriculture is profitable as long as it has access to cheap labour; it shares that characteristic with some of the modern forms of labour-intensive export industries. Cheap labour presupposes cheap food, which in some instances can be most readily obtained from imports. The development of commercialised export agriculture might contribute to the neglect of domestic food production both because attention and resources are concentrated on productivity improvement in the plantation (supply side effects) and because need for cheap food opens up the domestic market to cheap imports.

The political and economic dynamics of the long-term development of food production in Sri Lanka are illuminating. The plantation system was created alongside indigenous agriculture but with few linkages, utilising imported labour and management, and minimising the subsistence costs of labour through a cheap food import policy. While the vulnerability resulting from dependence on food imports brought the policy into question at the time of the First World War, it was only when the political system became responsive to the demands of indigenous farmers that a long process of structural change began. Sri Lankan dependence on food imports was reduced not by changing the product mix of the plantation sector, but rather by making more land available to the indigenous, small-scale farmers and increasing their productivity. The competing pressures to provide cheap food and support for food producers was managed by a complex process of food subsidies.

The case of plantation agriculture may be taken as illustrative of a more general set of pressures, both economic and political, for a cheap food policy. Export-oriented industry and mining may also need cheap labour, and therefore cheap food, while urban population growth gives rise to direct political pressures for cheap food price policies.

The examples discussed above relate to situations in which either limited foreign exchange constraints economic activity or the need to support a low cost export sector influences food policy. Quite a different situation exists in countries with booming export earnings, such as the oil exporters, or countries experiencing other mineral booms. In these countries, while there may be no particular need for cheap food imports, the economic consequences of the boom may create difficulties for domestic food production, as well as for other industries producing for the domestic market.

A favourable exchange rate and the lack of any pressing economic need to restrain imports strengthens competition from abroad. As the boom is likely to be associated with accelerated urbanisation and increasing sophistication in consumer tastes, the changing structure of food demand is likely to increase the competitive edge of the food importers.

At the same time, the expansion of urban employment and social welfare tightens the rural labour market, making it difficult to sustain agricultural production under a traditional labour-intensive regime. A conscious policy to inject capital and technology and to support prices may be necessary.

The discussion so far has been mainly concerned with the implications of international economic relations for commercial food production. Another important set of problems needs to be considered in relation to the indirect effects of exogenous economic influence on certain communities which remain virtually outside the international or even national economy. Pastoral nomads, hunters and gatherers, and other groups living in relatively inhospitable environmental conditions (at least from the point of view of the outside world) in many instances were left in only a marginal relationship to the national or international economy, insulated, in a sense, by their limited material resources.

It may well be that throughout history, crises resulting from essentially endogenous development have been endemic to some of these communities, but there can be little question that many contemporary examples of breakdown have resulted from exogenous pressures, or shocks, such as:

a) politically imposed constraints (e.g. 'sedentarisation' of nomads);

b) the encroachment of competing systems (e.g. the cultivation of dry season grazing);

c) environmental dislocation resulting from the overall pressure of development on the resource base;

d) the alienation of the resource base for other uses (e.g. intrusion of mining interests);

e) external impact on tastes and habits.

In these cases, the breakdown in food supply is a particularly brutal facet of a more general collapse in the face of the political, economic and cultural encroachment by the outside world (3).

4. SELF-SUFFICIENCY AND PRIORITY FOR DOMESTIC FOOD PRODUCTION

The preceding section has suggested that in many situations there may be a powerful impetus to encourage food imports where this is the readiest means of ensuring a supply of cheap food. How far is this socially justified? Neo-classical trade theory suggests that it is perfectly sound to acquire food through trade, if a country's comparative advantage is such that it can acquire more food by allocating its resources to the production of non-food exports and trading them for imported food. The formal logic of that case is excellent, despite the emotional appeal of arguments for food self-sufficiency. Grounds for disagreeing with such a view therefore need to be established with some care.

Before presenting such arguments, however, it may be useful to give two examples of circumstances in which there can be some agreement about the good sense of importing food.

One example is provided by countries whose boundaries are drawn in such a way as to make them dependent on food imports. In the case of Singapore, it would be as ludicrous to make the case for food self-sufficiency as it would be for Manhattan. If the extreme cases are excepted, there is necessarily a range of cases where varying degrees of dependence on imported food are reasonable at an intuitive level, without reference to the formal logic of neo-classical economics.

Nevertheless, it might be felt that the need for secure food supplies is such as to justify local production except in extreme conditions, in order to avoid the vagaries of world markets. In general, however, the natural supply uncertainties from any given limited geographical area are greater than uncertainty encountered at the world level, where natural risks are diversified. Indeed, it is precisely societies with a relatively low level of trade which are subject to the highest degree of food insecurity. In general, therefore, supply uncertainty does not seem to support the case for growing rather than trading.

Apart from purely strategic arguments, what are the general arguments for domestic food production, if any?

The economic arguments for special emphasis on food production as a means of securing food supplies may be grouped under three headings.

The first group of arguments, while accepting the logic of neo-classical comparative advantage theory, claims that as a result of "distortions" in exchange rates and pricing policies, the farmer is faced with costs and returns which do not reflect the social returns from food production and that corrective measures are therefore required.

The second line of argument goes beyond observed price "distortions" to suggest that intellectual error and vested urban interests are likely to result in both urban bias and bias in favour of export crops not only in price policies but also in public investment decisions and other public policies (e.g. research and extension). Only specific countermeasures are likely to result in food production receiving the priority it deserves on grounds of comparative advantage (4).

Thirdly, with respect to the longer-term distributional consequences of a shift by local farmers from food production, it has been argued that the growth of cash crop export production could lead to a polarisation among farmers, with the less successful ones becoming marginalised and landless. Moreover, even if, in principle, exports create the possibility of importing food, government policy and inadequacies in the distributional system may prevent imported food from taking the place of foregone local food production.

From the point of view of the smallholder, shifting to export crop production may also entail greater vulnerability to taxation, because export crops flow through centralised, controllable markets. If taxes are increased on export crops, there is little else the farmer can do with his output (except smuggle it), whereas food crops can be consumed in the household or sold locally in markets which are not readily controlled.

The validity of arguments about the distributional consequences of changes in the output mix in agriculture cannot be resolved by a priori reasoning but must be judged by empirical analysis. A related type of analysis suggests that food production is often below anticipated levels, given the resource endowment, because the rural institutional structure discourages optimal utilisation of land and labour (e.g. because of large-scale holdings of under-utilised land, or because of landlord or share-cropping systems). In that context land reform may be seen not only as a form of property (and ultimately income) redistribution but also as a means to achieve a more productive utilisation of available resources. Without land reform, increases in farm prices may well increase rents and solidify the position of landowners, rather than eliciting a supply response from the actual producers.

In addition to arguments which suggest that food production may not receive the attention it deserves, even in terms of narrow assessment of static comparative advantage, there is also a line of reasoning based on the expected longer-term global resource constraints on food production in a world of growing population and increasing pressure on the world's agricultural resources. It might therefore be sensible to extend food production beyond levels justifiable on the basis of contemporary production and trading possibilities, with a view to the longer-term returns to be expected from an expanded capacity to produce food.

In these terms, the anticipated economic returns from the pursuit of evident short-term comparative advantage have to be weighed against an evaluation of longer-term shifts in comparative advantage, as well as other strategic and social factors.

5. FOOD AND THE DEBATE ABOUT DEVELOPMENT STRATEGY

In over-simplified terms, the evolution of thinking regarding development policy might be separated into two periods. Up to the early 1960s, much of the literature envisaged development in terms of maximising growth through a process of industrialisation. The main topics of debate were the appropriate industrial strategy, the choice of techniques in industry and the means of sustaining high rates of capital formation. Progress was defined in terms of displacement of traditional activity as modern industrial production expanded. In relation to international trade, the priority was to reduce excessive dependence on primary commodity exports.

From the mid-1960s, the weight of opinion shifted. On the one hand, dramatic difficulties faced, for example, by India in her industrialisation efforts as a result of lagging agricultural production focussed attention on the need to give greater emphasis to the agricultural sector in order to sustain the momentum of growth. On the other hand, questioning about the goals of development policy concentrated attention on the distribution of the benefits of growth. Among other things, this lent support to a shift in the balance of the development effort towards the rural areas where the poor are concentrated. Food production therefore received much higher priority in the development agenda.

While the schematic presentation above may accurately reflect one aspect of reality, namely the climate of opinion among development economists, it does not reflect the more complex realities of policies in practice. A more valid impression of the evolution of development policy would have to rest on a number of qualifications:

a) even before opinions changed during the 1960s, many of the proponents of industrialisation (e.g. the structuralist school of the Economic Commission for Latin America) recognised that agricultural stagnation could act as a check on industrial progress, and land reform was indicated as a necessary component of the strategies they advocated;

b) accelerated technical progress in agriculture in the late 1960s and the 1970s resulted as much from an earlier commitment of resources to fundamental agricultural research (i.e. the development of the "new seeds"), as from a shift in policy objectives;

c) the shift in emphasis in the development literature has brought about only limited changes of policies.

The shift in the climate of opinion may well have deeper effects as it begins to influence the thinking of policy-makers in this decade. However, it should also be noted that, at the moment, policy-makers in most developing countries are more likely to be pushed by the harsh imperatives of the international economic crisis than the reform-mongering of development economists.

In this context, it may be more important to explore the role of agriculture in general and food production in particular in the adjustment to external shocks than to assess its role in the pursuit of distribution goals.

NOTES AND REFERENCES

1. Based on an unpublished paper by Dr. Brian van Arkadie, prepared while he held the position of Director of Research of the Development Centre.

2. The alternatives were perhaps most clearly articulated in the Soviet Industrialisation debate; the analysis of Preobrazhinsky remains a remarkably clear statement of the fundamental relationships between sectors.

3. See, for example, Brian Van Arkadie, "The Future of Vulnerable Societies", in Development and Change (Special Issue, January 1978).

4. Both these types of argument run through Michael Lipton's Why Poor People Stay Poor, A Study of Urban Bias in World Development, Temple Smith, London, 1977. The study also demonstrates that arguments in favour of emphasis on food production can also be arguments for income redistribution since increasing the return from food production is seen as a means of raising the real incomes of poor farmers and farm workers and even, Lipton argues, as a means of increasing the incomes of the urban poor (e.g. by reducing rural-urban migration and increasing the bargaining power of the urban poor). In particular, emphasis on food production can be seen as a direct means of combatting rural poverty.

Chapter II

IMPACT OF AGRICULTURAL EXPORT ACTIVITIES
ON THE DOMESTIC FOOD CHAIN

INTRODUCTION

Agricultural production by developing countries for export, mainly to countries in the North, has long been viewed as the logical way of making good economic use of the resource endowment of the South. The increasing difficulties of developing countries to meet their food requirements have led to mounting criticism of this view. Some seem to attribute a major share of responsibility for developing countries' food problems to export crop development (1). We shall examine in this chapter to what extent so critical a view is justified and which policy changes would be conducive to a more satisfactory situation. Of course, we do not assume that there is a single correct view and a unique set of solutions. Situations differ between countries and periods and a value judgement is implied in whatever role one attributes to a particular sector, i.e. agriculture.

Clarification is necessary at the outset with regard to terminology: the term food production or food crop production is used to describe production for domestic food consumption as opposed to production for export or export crop production. Where appropriate, a distinction is made between subsistence food production and food production for the domestic market. Therefore, export production can actually include food crops. To avoid confusion, we shall not use the term cash crop. When referring to other authors and statistics, however, exceptions to this rule may be inevitable.

1. HISTORICAL PERSPECTIVE

The introduction of export crops by the colonial powers more or less severely disrupted an agricultural system geared to satisfying nearly exclusively the food needs of the local populations in Africa and Asia (2). This does not mean that the traditional patterns of agriculture, hunting and gathering always provided abundant food, but that they formed a relatively closed system.

Its opening-up triggered otf a complex process which gathered momentum

27

over time and contributed to the pattern of agricultural development as it exists today, decades after the creation of politically independent nation states in most areas. How has the supply of food for domestic consumption been affected by the introduction and promotion of export crops?

Theoretically, in a situation with idle land and under-employed labour, one could imagine export crop production as a simple addition to existing agricultural production, resulting in a corresponding increase in material wealth. But this seems to have been the exception rather than the rule. Schematically, three types of attitudes can be distinguished among the colonial authorities (3). First, and perhaps most frequent was the attitude of taking food production for granted -- in other words, benign neglect, assuming sufficient resources to meet both export requirements and domestic food needs. Second, where the scarcity of resources was clearly perceived, priority was given to the export crop which was profitable enough to pay for food imports. This was the case in Sri Lanka (then Ceylon) where, in addition, labour was imported to work on the plantations. Rice, the staple food of this labour, was imported from other Asian colonies and a pattern of heavy import dependence was established. A third attitude, at the most exploitative end of the spectrum, consisted in suppressing local food production to support the food trade carried on by (foreign) traders and metropolitan producers while at the same time pressuring the local work force into plantations devoted to export crops. In other words, in order to oblige local labour to work in export crop production, their food production had to be made precarious and insufficient to meet their needs for a monetary income (4).

This schematic presentation obviously simplifies a complex reality where different attitudes exist at the same time and change over time. Official attitudes may be reinforced or counteracted in their effects by those with economic interests at stake: European settlers and traders on the one hand and farmers on the other hand. Thus, there are frequent references in the literature to the struggle of farmers to maintain food production, at least for their own consumption (5). The mechanisms used to promote export crops included economic incentives, administrative measures boycott and coercion. The ways in which some of these mechanisms have been implemented will be analysed in a later section of this chapter.

The pattern of introduction of export crops also varied with different types of producers. In the Ivory Coast, for example, foreign settlers created coffee or cocoa plantations as a monoculture, whereas African growers cultivated these export crops alongside their traditional food crops of plantain, yam, rice and cassava (6). Today, African growers still give priority to the food crops which are planted first. The young coffee and cocoa plants then benefit from the care given to the latter.

To demonstrate the impact of export crop production on food production in a historical perspective, it would be appropriate to compare time series of output, yield and resources used for the different crops. However, available data are notoriously weak, not only because of large components of subsistence production but also because the records of traded goods are unreliable (7). Where food production estimates are based on rural population data, one can expect a systematic upward bias in a situation of land scarcity and declining labour productivity. Having sounded this note of caution, it may nevertheless be useful to examine available time series on food production and agricultural exports.

FAO production indices over the period 1967-1981 show, in general, an almost parallel evolution of food production and total agricultural production (no separate indices are provided for non-food crops). This is striking at the global level, as well as for major developing regions. In fact, for nearly all years covered, the food production indices either equal or exceed the agricultural indices by up to two points (see Table 1). An exception to this general picture is the category "other developing market economies" (8) where, between 1973 and 1981, food production has consistently lagged behind agricultural production, but never by more than two index points. The evolution of production indices in Africa merits special attention. Whereas the near-parallelism between food and agriculture found elsewhere also holds true for this continent, the level of production clearly lags behind.

Understandably, the picture is less homogeneous for individual countries, and country-specific patterns are perceptible. Indices for selected countries provided in Table 2 are again almost parallel and generally show a slight advance of food production, particularly since the mid-1970s. For several years, in the period 1967-1973, food production indices in some countries (especially Ivory Coast, Tanzania, Mexico, Brazil) lagged behind. Korea is the only country among those listed where food production indices lagged more consistently and longer, i.e. until 1977.

On the country level, these figures certainly need careful interpretation which cannot be provided here (9). As presented, however, they are not consistent with the contention that there has been a general neglect of food production in developing countries.

Nevertheless, the growth in overall food production has been far from satisfactory, given the effective demand and nutritional needs of increasing populations. Although this inadequacy is generally recognised (10), analysis at the aggregate level is not very meaningful, particularly if one wants to know how specific groups of people and crops have been affected by the evolution of food production.

An analysis carried out by the FAO (11) of agricultural production in 90 developing countries (accounting for 90 per cent of total developing country population excluding China) over the years 1963-1975 distinguishes between cereals, other food crops and non-food crops. It shows annual growth rates for the first two categories of 2.7 and 2.9 per cent, but only 1.2 per cent for non-food crops. This set of statistics is inconsistent with the hypothesis of an overall neglect of food crop production in developing countries in favour of non-food crops. It again underlines the need for in-depth analysis on a country by country basis, and further disaggregation by product, socio-economic group and region.

Even though our data do not confirm the hypothesis that export crops have been substituted for food crops in a massive way and across the board, the food situation is clearly critical in many countries. Food demand in some countries has been increasing more rapidly than domestic supply due to population growth, rising incomes and increasing urbanisation. While domestic food supply may thus become more and more insufficient, agricultural exports may have been maintained or even increased. It is against this background

Table 1

INDICES OF FOOD AND AGRICULTURAL PRODUCTION AND OF AGRICULTURAL EXPORT VOLUME FOR MAJOR DEVELOPING REGIONS

(1969-71 = 100)

	1967	1968	1969	1970	1971	1972	1973	1974	1975	1976	1977	1978	1979	1980	1981
Developing M.E.															
Food	90	93	97	101	102	102	106	108	115	118	124	129	129	133	140
Agriculture	90	93	97	101	102	102	106	109	114	116	122	127	127	131	137
Agricultural exports	92	95	98	102	99	107	108	109	101	113	113	115	117	116	125
Africa															
Food	90	94	98	100	102	102	100	107	108	111	109	113	115	120	123
Agriculture	90	94	98	100	102	102	101	107	107	110	109	112	114	118	122
Agricultural exports	95	100	100	104	96	109	110	103	93	99	85	85	85	83	82
Latin America															
Food	92	93	96	102	102	103	106	112	116	122	127	132	135	139	146
Agriculture	93	93	97	101	102	103	106	113	115	118	125	130	133	135	143
Agricultural exports	91	93	100	103	98	104	107	100	104	114	119	124	127	122	136
Near East															
Food	93	97	99	99	103	109	104	114	121	128	125	132	134	138	141
Agriculture	93	96	99	98	103	109	104	114	118	125	123	129	130	133	136
Agricultural exports	89	89	94	102	104	111	114	85	85	102	93	108	90	86	97
Far East															
Food	87	92	97	102	102	99	108	105	115	115	127	132	129	133	142
Agriculture	88	92	97	101	102	100	108	106	114	114	126	131	129	132	140
Agricultural exports	95	99	95	99	106	111	109	106	112	134	136	131	142	150	157
Other Developing															
Food	93	96	98	100	102	103	106	110	113	117	116	119	125	125	128
Agriculture	92	95	98	100	102	103	107	112	114	118	118	121	127	128	131
Agriculture exports	80	94	99	99	103	97	95	98	106	103	119	113	128	131	127
World															
Food	94	97	97	100	103	103	108	110	114	116	119	124	125	125	129
Agriculture	94	97	97	100	103	103	108	110	113	115	118	123	124	124	128

Source: FAO, Production Yearbooks and Trade Yearbooks, various years.

Table 2

INDICES OF FOOD AND AGRICULTURAL PRODUCTION FOR SELECTED DEVELOPING COUNTRIES (1969-71 = 100)

	1967	1968	1969	1970	1971	1972	1973	1974	1975	1976	1977	1978	1979	1980	1981
Algeria															
Food	86	101	96	103	101	104	94	99	102	112	90	97	103	120	120
Agriculture	86	101	96	103	101	104	95	99	102	112	90	98	103	120	120
Egypt															
Food	86	97	98	99	103	105	105	106	110	113	108	112	114	117	116
Agriculture	86	94	99	99	102	104	103	102	103	106	103	107	110	114	113
Ghana															
Food	91	89	95	101	104	100	103	115	108	99	91	92	99	100	100
Agriculture	91	89	95	101	104	101	103	115	108	99	91	92	99	99	100
Ivory Coast															
Food	86	87	94	97	109	107	112	127	136	135	136	144	154	166	176
Agriculture	78	94	93	101	106	108	116	117	131	134	133	131	147	154	171
Nigeria															
Food	86	89	100	102	98	100	94	103	106	109	110	114	119	126	129
Agriculture	86	88	100	102	98	100	94	102	106	109	110	113	118	125	128
Tanzania															
Food	90	91	95	105	100	100	101	100	104	113	118	121	122	121	124
Agriculture	92	91	97	104	99	101	101	100	104	112	113	115	116	116	120
Zambia															
Food	95	95	97	95	108	109	107	121	125	135	130	130	117	123	135
Agriculture	95	96	97	95	108	109	108	120	125	133	129	128	116	123	134
Mexico															
Food	93	95	95	100	105	108	111	114	116	116	128	140	133	145	155
Agriculture	94	98	96	100	105	107	110	115	113	113	126	137	131	141	150
Brazil															
Food	88	91	94	102	104	107	112	123	129	142	147	141	150	165	172
Agriculture	91	91	97	98	105	109	108	123	124	125	136	134	142	152	165
Peru															
Food	92	83	94	102	104	104	107	112	109	111	111	106	109	100	112
Agriculture	92	86	95	102	104	102	107	110	106	108	109	106	111	102	112
Bangladesh															
Food	99	101	107	101	92	91	102	98	109	103	112	116	117	124	121
Agriculture	100	101	108	102	90	92	102	96	106	101	111	115	116	121	118
India															
Food	87	91	96	102	102	97	106	99	113	110	124	128	121	126	135
Agriculture	88	91	96	102	103	98	106	100	113	110	124	128	121	126	134
Korea (Republic of)															
Food	86	86	100	99	101	102	105	112	122	130	155	163	163	136	157
Agriculture	86	87	100	99	101	104	107	114	123	132	156	163	163	136	155
Portugal															
Food	98	100	97	105	98	93	98	99	99	95	80	80	93	83	69
Agriculture	99	105	97	105	98	93	97	99	99	95	80	81	93	84	70

Source: FAO, Production Yearbooks, various years.

31

that export production is sometimes blamed for food deficits. Yet the statistical evidence hardly bears this out; comparison of the indices of agricultural production and of agricultural export volume shows that the export volume has grown more slowly than agricultural production for developing market economies as a group. This is very clear for the years 1974-1979, whereas in the preceding seven years agricultural export indices tended to be slightly higher than those of agricultural production (see Table 1). The picture is even more striking for certain developing regions. For Africa, for example, the agricultural export index exceeded the production index until 1973 but then diminished, not only in relative but also in absolute terms. The interpretation of these changes is difficult. Do they reflect the resistance of the food production system? Are they related to changes in export markets and the taxation of exports? Or did civil strife hamper exports to a point where the indices were affected?

Despite the data weaknesses, it would appear that the growth of export crops cannot, in general, be made responsible for growing good deficits in the second half of the 1970s, although in some countries and in specific circumstances, export crop production may well have had an adverse effect on food production.

The following section will elaborate on the difficult question of the developmental role of agricultural exports in many poor developing countries.

2. THE DEVELOPMENTAL ROLE OF AGRICULTURAL EXPORTS

The role agricultural exports can play in the development process depends not only on the resource endowment of a country but also on its socio-economic structure and on the potential export market. The role it should play is more a question of the development objectives pursued. Given natural resources, comparative advantage and export markets, the potential role ranges from "engine of development" at one end to "obstacle to development" at the other (12).

In the first case, agricultural exports procure the foreign exchange which is used to increase productivity both in agriculture and in other sectors of the economy. The benefits of exports are widely spread and mutually reinforcing: increased productivity in the urban sector will increase and diversify demand for agricultural products; the agricultural sector will in turn benefit from an increased and possibly cheaper supply of non-agricultural products. In this ideal scenario, infrastructural improvements and better health and education services will accompany the growth of export agriculture and no group of the population will be excluded (directly or indirectly) from sharing in the benefits.

Agricultural exports can continue to play a stimulating role in sequences of increased income, investment and consumption as long as the resource base and external demand permit and the internal balance of distribution and socio-economic structure is maintained. In this scenario, export crop production may be developed as a complement to food production or at its expense. In the latter case, it would not reduce food availability but rather secure its supply through low-cost imports.

At the other end of the spectrum is the scenario in which export crop production becomes an obstacle to development. In fact, it is not export crop production as such, but the conditions under which it is promoted and the use to which foreign exchange receipts are put which can turn it into an obstacle. A socially doubtful process of development may be engendered, with the benefits appropriated mainly by the big producers and traders. Government may play an important role in determining the distribution of export benefits. Where State trading companies play a dominant role, only a small share of the export receipts may actually be passed on to the producers (13). In this case, not only is the general economic stimulation effect likely to be weak, it will also bring about the conditions for a dual economy and society characterised by economic inefficiency, social injustice and, perhaps in the longer run, political instability.

Development based on export crop production may be limited even further by the way in which the receipts are appropriated and used. If, for example, they are spent largely on luxury consumption or military hardware, they will most likely increase imports without any positive effect on production and productivity in the domestic economy. If agricultural producers feel that they carry an undue share of the burden of such development, they will tend to limit their export crop production and switch to food production to the extent feasible. However, this is not always possible and migration to urban centres may be seen as the best way to escape the pressure. Thus, rural-urban migration, which may be occurring for a number of reasons, can be reinforced and food producers, however marginal, will increase the ranks of urban consumers. Domestic agriculture may be increasingly unable to satisfy the urban demand for food and food imports will grow, not because of any comparative disadvantage of domestic producers but because the use of export receipts from agriculture gradually destroys the agricultural sector and eventually the whole economy. While one may expect forces of self-correction to operate in a market economy, these forces can be thwarted by the actions of private traders and by government policies.

The two scenarios outlined above represent extreme cases, and reality is more likely to be somewhere in between. Socio-economic structures and government policies will determine the actual mix of stimulating and disrupting effects caused by export agriculture. Conflicts of interest are not easily arbitrated by governments anywhere, and governments themselves are rarely without internal conflict. For example, the Minister of Finance may tend to favour a certain type of export agriculture because of its short-term fiscal benefits, whereas the Minister of Agriculture, with prime responsibility for long-term food supply and as a spokesman for the interests of the rural community, may prefer a more diversified agricultural structure.

Thus, depending on the circumstances, a strategy based on export agricultural may be successful, economically and socially. Nevertheless, some authors insist that it is inherently evil and part of an international conspiracy to exploit developing countries in general and agricultural producers in particular (14). It is true that export agriculture creates opportunities for abuse at various levels which do not exist in a system of subsistence agriculture. Trade always implies dependence on markets. And when the markets are foreign, governments tend to be involved as the authority regulating exports and imports. Furthermore, heavy reliance on markets characterised by important swings involves risks which countries would want to avoid. However, while abuse of the export production system can indeed jeopardize a country's food security as outlined above, ways and means can be found to prevent such abuse. We shall elaborate on this in the final section of this chapter.

The risk of dependence through agricultural export production merits further analysis. Seen against the objective of food security, the question is whether agricultural export production increases the risk of a shortfall in food availability. This question arises only where domestic food production is replaced by agricultural export production. If the latter is considered economically advantageous at the moment of its introduction, three sets of questions must nevertheless be asked. First, will the foreign exchange earned from such exports actually be used for food imports to the extent necessary to make up for the loss in domestic food production? Second, if an adequate quantity of food is being imported, will it be distributed in such a way that availability at the consumer level for all major categories of the population will be at least as high, timely and cheap as it would have been with domestic production? Third, what are the risks of changes over time in the factors which determine food import capacity? The following are among the factors to be examined:

a) Vulnerability of non-food agricultural export production (as compared to food production) due to disease and weather conditions; this may be particularly important if export crops are produced as a monoculture;

b) Demand prospects on the world market, including international competitiveness, conditions of access to export markets and possibilities for substitution;

c) Price fluctuations for both export crops and food products to be imported;

d) Time required for the domestic agricultural system to adjust if the above factors evolve in such a way as to jeopardize adequate export receipts.

The result of the examination of these issues will determine whether export dependence can be justified on the grounds that the export receipts contribute to development without reducing food availability.

Developing countries do not have identical options with respect to sources of foreign exchange. Those with little other than agricultural resources will have to rely on export crops to some extent in any case, and it may only be a question of which ones to select for promotion. Table 3 shows the large differences in the share of agricultural products in the exports of selected developing countries (15). In the majority of the countries listed, agriculture is still carrying more than 50 per cent of the burden of earning foreign exchange which is used largely for non-agricultural purposes. As long as food requirements are being met, either by domestic production or with the help of imports, these foreign exchange earnings from agriculture may appear not only desirable but even crucial for development.

However, it has been argued that the value of such foreign exchange earnings is exaggerated and that a more self-reliant development model in all respects -- including consumption patterns, production technologies, energy

Table 3

SHARE OF AGRICULTURAL EXPORTS IN TOTAL EXPORTS
IN SELECTED DEVELOPING COUNTRIES (1)

(in 1978 if not stated otherwise)

Above 40 per cent			Below 10 per cent		
Afghanistan	66.5	(1977)	Algeria	0.4	
Argentina	41.4		Bolivia	4.8	(1973)
Benin	61.0	(1974)	Chile	8.4	(1977)
Burundi	95.3	(1976)	Iran	1.4	(1976)
Cameroon	73.7	(1979)	Iraq	0.8	(1976)
Central African Rep.	48.3		Jamaica	5.3	
Chad	73.3	(1975)	Korea	6.7	
Colombia	72.7	(1977)	Nigeria	4.9	(1977)
Costa Rica	58.1		Senegal	9.8	(1974)
El Salvador	53.4		Tunisia	5.3	
Ethiopia	79.1	(1976)	Venezuela	0.9	(1977)
Ghana	70.1	(1977)	Zambia	1.5	(1977)
Guatemala	68.9	(1977)			
Haiti	49.8	(1977)			
Ivory Coast	70.6				
Kenya	58.8				
Madagascar	80.0				
Malawi	83.2				
Mali	88.3	(1976)			
Mozambique	45.4	(1975)			
Nicaragua	58.9				
Paraguay	53.1	(1976)			
Rwanda	77.2	(1976)			
Somalia	80.7	(1976)			
Sri Lanka	69.7	(1979)			
Sudan	91.7	(1976)			
Tanzania	74.1	(1976)			
Uganda	94.6	(1976)			
Upper Volta	84.0	(1975)			

1.   Only countries with a population above one million are listed.

Source: UN 1979 Yearbook of International Trade Statistics.

use, and even medicine -- would considerably reduce the burden placed on the agricultural producers. While such views require consideration, we find that the proposition is more constructively analysed by an examination of the particular circumstances, by crop and by country, in respect of the factors of dependence listed above. The options actually available will depend not only on economic opportunities but also on the socio-political capacity for rational choice and for implementing the strategy and policies adopted.

3. MECHANISMS AND CHARACTERISTICS OF EXPORT CROP DEVELOPMENT

Whatever role one wants to attribute to export crops, it is important to assess their patterns of change, for although there is no single pattern, and the forces and mechanism of changes vary with different crops, countries and over time, some frequently-encountered patterns may be identified.

a) Substitution among crops

Except for the rare cases where there are unutilised resources of land, labour and other inputs, it is usually assumed that export crop development takes place at the expense of food crops. However, such substitution between crops is not always easy to track. It may be a matter of acreage planted with different crops, or of the uses made of labour or other inputs, or finally, and perhaps more frequently, it may involve acreage, labour and other inputs all being shifted from one crop to another. However, this is unlikely to follow a fixed pattern; there will usually be differences according to the region, the size of the farm, the farming system and other factors.

Furthermore, in a dynamic setting, product substitution does not necessarily take the form of a reduction in the level of use of any input but may be reflected in growth rate differentials. This was the case, for example, in the Ivory Coast during the 1970s, when the production of export crops and of food crops increased simultaneously. Sometimes food crop production virtually stagnates or grows slowly, while export crop production grows rapidly. In Brazil, for example, soybean production increased tenfold between 1970 and 1980, while the production of dry beans declined by about 7.5 per cent and that of rice increased by 30 per cent (16). Similarly, in Mali, the doubling of cotton production between 1969-71 and 1981 was accompanied by a 15 per cent rise in cereals output over the same period (17).

Changes in levels of output are frequent and sometimes large for export crops. The analysis of crop substitution patterns therefore has to concentrate on the causes of these changes, including factors such as area harvested and use of labour and other inputs. Unfortunately, on a crop basis, only acreage data are readily available; the use of other resources is generally not reported (18). It may be tempting to use yields as a proxy for other inputs, but this would be acceptable only if allowance could be made for other major factors influencing yields, e.g. weather, pests and land quality.

Conclusions drawn from statistical analysis of one factor alone, e.g. area harvested, may well be erroneous. Thus, if the best land is increasingly concentrated on a given crop, the output may increase even though the area harvested remains unchanged (19). Similarly, an increase in the area devoted to a given food crop does not guarantee that there is no crop substitution underway; increasingly extensive food production on deteriorating land (accompanied by labour out-migration) could explain why food production stagnates or declines even while the area harvested increases (20).

Since substitution between crops is less straightforward than often suggested, it is not surprising that contradictory views appear in the literature, probably reflecting differences in the underlying definitions or unwarranted generalisations. The limitations of the data used, in particular with regard to their regional, historical or crop specificity, must be kept in mind when drawing conclusions on this issue, even within a given country. In the case of Brazil, for example, Lester Brown maintains that "soybeans for animal feeding are bidding land away from table beans" (21). However, a look at the FAO production data for Brazil suggests that, except perhaps for specific local situations, the substitution in terms of land must have been relative rather than absolute. Over the period 1961-65 to 1977, the area harvested with pulses increased by 54 per cent, whereas the soybean area (although from a lower base) increased by nearly 2000 per cent.

b) Channels of change

The development of export crops may be explained in terms of the forces driving the economy, i.e. the pursuit of personal income and of governmental objectives, the development "ideology" and the relations between various actors. While in the end everything could probably be traced back to economic and social power relationships, it would appear useful to review the channels of change in their real world configurations, concentrating on concrete specific matters, such as research, infrastructure and the role of agro-industry.

The manner in which and the extent to which the natural resource base of land and people is deployed depends on economic and social choices, which are themselves determined by a complex and interdependent set of factors. It is therefore very difficult to distinguish and assess the impact of the many technical, economic and social factors which impinge on export crop development. While there is a certain degree of arbitrariness in any classification, we proceed in the following sections to discuss export crop development in the three categories most frequently highlighted in the literature.

c) Research

Research is a major component of the food production system. It determines to a considerable extent present levels of productivity and is decisive for the exploitation of the production potential for the future.

The increase in food production in developing countries up to the 1960s may be explained without much reference to the application of research results to food crops as research was preponderantly concentrated on the major export crops (22). Colonial powers created research organisations for specific export crops, such as the British Cotton Research Corporation (abolished in 1975) and the West African Institute for Oil Palm Research (WAIFOR). The equivalent French research organisation, the Institut de Recherches pour les Huiles et Oléagineux (IRHO) was created in 1947. These institutions were quite succesful in promoting production through varietal improvement and plant protection (23).

The network of International Agricultural Research Centres (see Table 4), supported by the Consultative Group on International Agricultural Research (CGIAR), continued the crop-specific research, but with the creation of the International Rice Research Institute (IRRI) in the Philippines in 1960, the emphasis clearly shifted to food crops and livestock.

Table 4

INTERNATIONAL AGRICULTURAL RESEARCH CENTRES, 1979 (1)

Center and Starting Data (2)		Principal Location	Major Programmes	Senior Total	Staff Posts Soc. Sci.	1979 Budget ($ millions)
IRRI	1960	Philippines	Rice	58	6	13.2
CDIMYT	1966	Mexico	Wheat, Maize	75	6	14.7
IITA	1968	Nigeria	Systems, grains, legumes, tubers	95	2	12.9
CIAT	1968	Colombia	Forage-beef, field beans, cassava	61	4	12.5
WARDA	1971	Liberia	Rice	n.a.	n.a.	2.1
CIP	1972	Peru	Potatoes	29	3	7.2
ICRISAT	1972	India	Sorghum, Millet, groundnuts, dryland systems	60	7	9.0
IBPGR	1973	Italy	Genetic material	n.a.	n.a.	2.7
ILRAD	1974	Kenya	Trypanosomiasis	51	0	7.6
ILCA	1974	Ethiopia	Livestock production systems	44	13	7.0
IFPRI	1975	United States	Food Policies	20	20	2.0
ICARDA	1976	Syria	Crop and mixed farming systems	45	2	8.8
						$100.0 (rounded)

1. In addition to the 12 institutions listed two more centers are associated with but not directly supported by the CGIAR: Asian Vegetable Research and Development Center, Taiwan, 1971, and International Fertilizer Development Center, United States, 1975.

2. Full designation of centers are:

IRRI: International Rice Research Institute
CDIMYT: International Maize and Wheat Improvement Center
IITA: International Institute of Tropical Agriculture
WARDA: West Africa Rice Development Association
CIP: International Potato Center
ICRISAT: International Crop Research Institute for the Semi-Arid Tropics

IBPGR: International Board for Plant Genetic Resources
ILRAD: International Laboratory for Research on Animal Diseases
ILCA: International Livestock Center for Africa
IFPRI: International Food Policy Research Institute
ICARDA: International Center for Agricultural Research in Dry Areas

Source: Haldore Hanson et al., "Plant and Animal Resources for Food Production by Developing Countries in the 1980's", paper prepared for a Conferencee on agricultural production, Bonn, Fed. Rep. of Germany, 8-12 October 1979.

It is obvious that, in the early days, economic and trade opportunities were responsible for the concentration of research on a few export crops. The results of this research, which continues in a variety of institutions, gives export crops a competitive edge over food crops. Since it takes a long time before research results of practical applicability are available, it may be some time before food crops have made up the lag; moreover, many of them are still held back by lack of financial and technological support.

To emphasize the role of research as an explanatory factor for crop development is not to suggest that there need be incompatibility between food crop and export crop research in the future; in fact, these two research orientations may become increasingly mutually-supportive. The dividing line does not necessarily lie between the two categories of food and export crops; it is as likely to be within each category, i.e. between different food crops and between different export crops. In fact, any such dividing line is determined by the system of reward and punishment facing the researcher and his financier, and this system is man-made and can be altered by public policy and decision. It is largely up to governments, therefore, individually and collectively, to decide whether to direct efforts more towards the food problems of developing countries than is the case today.

d) Extension, input supply and infrastructure

These are major components of the production support system, aiming mainly at increased yields but also at the introduction of new crops and the expansion of acreage planted.

Historically, extension, input supply and infrastructure have often been successfully organised to support specific export crops (24). The general assumption was that food would be produced in any case and therefore that support could be concentrated on crops which would earn foreign exchange and fiscal revenue (via export taxes) for the government. In practice, the relative emphasis on the promotion of export crops continues in many countries, even though it may now be less openly admitted in view of the pressing problems in the food sector. An illustration is provided by the neglect of food crops in investment allocations in the development plans of Tunisia, the Ivory Coast and Cameroon (25). In Cameroon, the 1976-1981 Plan provided allocations for investment in agriculture as follows: 60 per cent for projects involving exclusively export crops; 9 per cent for projects involving mainly export crops, but including a food crop component; 25 per cent for food crop production and agro-industry; and 6 per cent for miscellaneous infrastructure. For Tunisia and the Ivory Coast, the situation is comparable.

Similarly, with regard to input supply, preference tends to be given to export crops (for example, cotton in Egypt). But if farmers see a possibility of using the inputs more profitably for other crops (e.g. vegetables) they do so and thus counteract government production planning (26). The picture is again the same for extension services. In Chad, for instance, the extension service recommends direct fertilization only for cotton; thanks to crop rotation, sorghum may benefit from a residual impact (27). Given this orientation of the support services, input supplies are often organised cropwise.

Discrimination of the production support system in favour of export crops may be explained by both technical and economic reasons. Concentration on one crop, so the argument goes, is technically simpler and economically more profitable. But these arguments are not always valid. In many cases, food crops and export crops (especially coffee and cocoa) are complementary in terms of land and labour requirements. Mixed cropping can even be technically and economically superior to monoculture (28).

e) Agro-industry

Agro-industry is another major force in export crop development (29). It can enhance crop production through the supply of inputs and services on the one hand and by offering a market on the other hand. Where it enjoys a monopsonist position the danger that it may abuse its power is particularly great. The terms on which agro-industry deals with agricultural producers have to be analysed in individual cases to clarify the real effects. Distortion of the production pattern and strengthening of a particular part of the agricultural sector may in fact go hand in hand. The intervention of multinational corporations in export crop development is generally characterised by, and criticised for, its disregard for the satisfaction of food needs of the local population and the disruption of existing socio-economic patterns (30). Yet such disregard and disruption are not inherent in the operation of the multinational corporate organisation of production. Nevertheless, even though multinational firms may in fact have played a supportive role in the food systems in Pakistan and in some Latin American countries, the monopolistic power of the multinational corporations in practice tends to represent a force for inequity in developing countries where there is little or no effective countervailing power of the kind that operates in industrialised countries (31). It has been convincibly argued that agro-industry contributes to an undesirable export bias in agricultural development in Brazil and Venezuela due to pricing practices (transfer prices) which transfer productivity gains out of the country.

f) Prices and marketing

The price mechanism provides the main production and marketing signals in export crop development within an open economy. Price elasticity of supply is generally poositive and can be quite high for a single crop if other crop prices remain stable or change less (33). Thus, relatively high prices for export crops promote export crop development rather than food crop production. In addition, marketing of export crops is generally well organised. Under the circumstances, producers tend to respond to prices and market signals by switching to export crops as quickly and as extensively as they can. The country will then experience a commensurate foreign exchange gain.

However, this simple presentation of the beneficial effects of the price mechanism suffers from the weakness that the argument hinges on the ability of producers effectively to increase or decrease export crop production as prices vary. Furthermore, prices at the farm level do not directly reflect those in the export and import market. While the pricing and marketing systems may indeed offer incentives for increased production (e.g. high and stable prices), there are also circumstances in which the benefits of price changes accrue to those who organise and control the trade while the costs are borne by the producers. For example, if farmers need cash income, say, to pay taxes, but cannot find a sufficiently large market for their food crops (because of lack of effective demand), export crop production may represent the only alternative. And when the obligation to pay taxes is abolished, as for example in Togo in 1974, the pressure may continue in other forms (34). More generally, a growing desire to buy manufactured products may induce increased export crop production. Indebtedness (particularly if it is characterised by usurious rates) may also force producers to increase their market production. When, for example, a farmer has to borrow money to buy food during a period of crop failure, the repayment obligation may compel him to produce more export crops in the following season. For many farmers in developing countries, indebtedness is perpetuated and even increased up to the point where they have to sell their land. They may then continue their precarious existence as agricultural labourers or migrate to urban areas.

In an analysis of the case of Sudan, Wohlmuth and Oesterdiekhoff (35) conclude that where subsistence food production coexists with export production, agriculture can be permanently squeezed without necessarily leading to the collapse we have described. The explanation is that when exposed to continued pressure, the remuneration of labour in export production can approach zero as long as subsistence production is sufficient for labour reproduction.

The marketing sytem itself may be so designed and operated that it brings about an inequitable distribution of gains from export production and trade as between farmers and traders, industry and government. The basic force is the exercise of power, be it legal (for example, government monopoly to export) or market power held by private traders. By keeping procurement prices low (in relation to marketing costs and world market prices) the government may appropriate a surplus which it may use and in fact often does use outside the agricultural sector. If farmers are unable to switch to other crops or to alternative markets (e.g. to smuggling), they are trapped by this kind of marketing arrangement. Governments often use intermediaries for the collection of export crops. In this case, as well as when they operate on their own behalf, private traders can use their market position to depress the price paid to producers, even where minimum prices have been announced (36). As a result, a fourfold exploitation of producers may be imposed through the price and marketing mechanisms: 1) monopolistic or oligopolistic pricing for inputs and usurious loans, 2) depressed buying price paid by middlemen, 3) government procurement price allowing for fiscal revenue, 4) deteriorating terms of trade in the international market (37).

It follows -- in theory as well as in practice -- that an improvement at one level, for example better international terms of trade, may be offset at another level, e.g. by government or private traders, and thus may not be passed on to the producers. A general increase in commodity prices in international trade is therefore not necessarily an effective means to help the rural poor (38). Consequently, the analysis of the impact of price policies has to cover the entire marketing chain and should not be limited to a single level.

While markets are influenced by power relationships which may bias resource allocation against the weaker members of the economy, judicious "manipulation" of prices and marketing sytems may also help to strengthen agriculture. For example, surpluses accumulated by the crop stabilisation fund in the Ivory Coast from the export of coffee, cocoa and palm oil were used to develop cotton production until 1973 (39). In a similar way, food production could be supported with surpluses from export crops.

Price policy is often the government's most important single instrument to influence the agricultural production pattern. But it is also an extremely difficult instrument to use judiciously and effectively because of the strong group interests involved and the need to anticipate and meet the reactions of producers, consumers and traders.

g) Social implications

Export crop development is frequently said to entail three major social implications: promotion of large producers; creation of regional imbalances; and reinforcement of the urban bias in development (40). While the mechanisms leading to such consequences have been referred to above, some further analysis is necessary if one considers that they may jeaopardize the developmental role of export crop production.

The literature provides mostly negative examples of social implications, i.e. cases where socio-economic inequality is increased by export crop development. Immediately efficiency considerations in the supply of inputs, in the administration of loans and in marketing often explain the virtual exclusion of small producers. As a result their productivity as independent producers remains low and their incomes may also be lower than those earned by workers on the large farms (41). Their vulnerability is such that one or two seasons of poor harvest may force them into heavy debts, from which they may not be able to extricate themselves, and which eventually oblige them to sell their land (42).

Discrimination against food crops (produced by small farmers) in the case of Brazil "results in a displacement of small units to the interior of the country and at the same time in an expulsion of farm workers due to the increasing use of modern inputs and mechanisation on larger farms` producing inputs for agro-industries and for foreign markets" (43). Migration to poorer land can thus be accompanied by rural-urban migration. The result is an increasing polarisation of the society, not only between urban and rural areas but also within the agricultural sector and between regions. This is reflected in income differentials and in the orientation of the modern sector (including export agriculture) which is "geared to the provision of goods for an elite" (44). A particular concern related to increased monetisation through export crop development is the effect on the intra-household distribution of income and on the expenditure pattern of monetary income. If, for example, export crops have substituted for subsistence crops and the farmer's cash income is not used for buying food, negative nutritional consequences may result despite adequate household income.

It appears that increased inequality as a result of export crop production is widespread. But there are also examples where the benefits from export crop production are very widely distributed. For example, in the Ivory Coast, Sawadogo reports that nearly one million households (i.e. over 90 per cent in major producing areas) own plots of coffee and cocoa trees (45). An even distribution of the necessary production assets and general access to necessary services, or remunerative employment possibilities in non-agricultural sectors, are therefore crucial to avoid negative social consequences from export crop development.

Where these conditions are not fulfilled, ways and means have to be found to introduce either countervailing power by the formation of groups of small farmers or government measures which prevent the unhindered play of economic power to squeeze or displace small producers. While the objective of such measures will be to further social injustice, they cannot be pushed to the point where efficiency is sacrificed beyond economically sustainable levels. While this is a real danger in certain cases, it is not necessarily linked or limited to export crop development; the resolution of this problem clearly lies beyond issues of agricultural policy.

4. MITIGATING DISTORTIONS AND EXPORT DEPENDENCE

We have seen that export crop development cannot reasonably be made responsible, either generally or exclusively, for the growing food deficits of developing countries. However, the situation varies from country to country over time. We have reviewed some of the evidence and mechanisms of adverse effects of agricultural exports on the domestic food chain in order to examine the hypothesis of export bias more concretely. Only a few cases are reported in the literature rather than reflecting the overall merits of export crop development.

In order to draw constructive conclusions from this heterogeneous body of evidence, one has to ask to what extent the adverse effects of export crops on the food chain are inevitable and how greater compatibility or mutual support between food crops and export crops can be achieved. The resource endowment and policy orientations will determine the concrete answers in specific cases, but some general discussion may be given of directions in which to search.

The discussion tends to centre on the possible dichotomy between food crops and export crops, and thus perhaps to overstate the degree of conflict. It is clearly not sufficient to look only at export crops when difficulties exist all along the food chain. Algeria provides an example where grain production has been falling over the last 25 years while major agricultural exports (wine, fruits and vegetables) have declined at the same time (46). In this and other cases, therefore, analysis of the food problem must take into account the country's entire development pattern and its relation to the food sector (47).

Scarcity of land and water and the existing technology may, in the short run, place food and export crops in direct competition. One crop can only progress at the expense of the other. In such circumstances, compatibility between competing crops can only be achieved in the longer run, with appropriate improvements in technology. To bring this about, initiative and perseverance at the political level are needed.

With existing technology and fully utilised resources, the arbitration between different crops takes place, in theory, via the prices offered to producers and the concrete marketing possibilities. In addition, as we have seen, power relationships (exercised by government, agro-industry, traders and money-lenders) influence production decisions and thus the entire food chain. Therefore, with or without a change in market prices, a change in these power relationships can mitigate distortions which may have been introduced in favour of export crops. A change in government policy depends basically on policy-makers' awareness of the general nature of the food system and its problems, and of the need to consider not only volumes of production, consumption, imports and exports but also the interests, actions and power of groups of producers, consumers and various intermediaries.

Once the government has drawn up the main outlines of its development strategy, the implications for imports and exports are largely determined. If it is felt that export crop production would have distorting effects on the food system, one way of mitigating them might be to reduce activity in this sub-sector and thus also gear the development pattern to a correspondingly lower level of imports for invetment or consumption or both. Foreign assistance may help to smooth such a transition. A gradual change in strategy is likely to be easier than a radical one. An example of a gradual approach may be seen in the Ivory Coast which has put greater emphasis than before on food crops in its 1981-1985 Development Plan (48).

Another type of distortion and dependence connected with export agriculture results from concentration on one or a few crops. Fluctuations of yields and of prices in international markets, combined, perhaps, with generally deteriorating terms of trade, all tend to adversely affect the income of producers and to reduce the effective demand for food. In such circumstances the remedy may lie in diversification of export crop production (where ecological and economic conditions permit) while maintaining its overall foreign exchange earning capacity. If diversification were to include food crops which are also consumed domestically, the domestic food sytem can be protected to some extent from fluctuations in production and world market conditions by making provisions for adequate domestic food security; this is, for example, the justification for the control of rice exports from Thailand.

Whatever change in the production pattern may seem desirable in order to mitigate existing distortions and dependencies resulting from export crop production, the concrete measures to be taken need to be designed with a view to their combined effect on the entire production support and output delivery systems for the various crops. It may be possible to integrate these systems; if not, discrimination should be avoided. An effort along these lines was made, for example, in Sri Lanka after the nationalisation of tea plantations in 1975 (49).

A gradual change in the production pattern will be easier where natural and economic conditions permit the simultaneous growth of food crop and export crop production. This seems to be possible in many areas of the humid tropics, for instance by associating cocoa and plantain bananas, coffee and rainfed rice, oil palm and cassava in African countries (50). In a similar vein, Togo plans to combine cattle raising and oil palm production (51). This is only possible when there are under-utilised resources and/or scope for intensification and technological change. However, it should be recalled that a technical success of this kind does not preclude (and may actually offer increased scope for) squeezing export crop producers (52). Where this is a real danger, there may be a need for reconsideration of the overall development strategy itself.

Finally, the distortion in the food system that may result from concentrating export crop production on only a few large producers can be mitigated by assuring wider participation in production, in particular by poorer people. This is no easy task, given the resistance of the now privileged beneficiaries of the system. Yet if no comparable, alternative sources of income exist, ways and means will have to be found to open up export agriculture to larger numbers of rural people. Increased income from export crops will increase the effective demand for food and may actually stimulate domestic food production. The greater the extent to which world market prices are passed on to the producers, the more successful such a strategy will be.

The justifications for different attempts to mitigate distortions and dependencies can be many. The following five kinds of arguments are most frequently put forward and will have to be examined before a change in policy is actually recommended. It is postulated, first, that export crop production does not always make the best use of existing resources; second, that certain socio-economic groups are marginalised by export crop production; third, that the satisfaction of nutritional needs is jeopardized by export crop production; fourth, that export crop production entails environmental damage and other social costs (e.g. of rapid urbanisation); and, finally, that it creates undue dependence on the outside world. This dependence is of a double nature: on the one hand, dependence for food imports on the world (food grain) market, which has experienced considerable fluctuations in recent years and which is supplied mainly by North America and a few other countries and operated by a small number of firms (53).

The various arguments may point in different directions and conflict with one another. For example, arguments in favour of economic profitability may indicate an expansion of export crop production, while those relating to social impact and external dependence may suggest containment rather than expansion. In weighing such arguments against each other, a careful look must be taken at the underlying assumptions and at the "real world" conditions of the economy under consideration. It may be unrealistic always to rely on the national government as a "neutral power broker", but institutional arrangements and mechanisms may be established so that the different points of view are at least heard, if not fully accommodated in a consistent fashion. In practice, the resulting compromise will rarely be formally agreed but more often established gradually as a result of different forces and constraints.

Improved knowledge on the operation of agro-business firms, for example, can help to inform the decisions made and strengthen the bargaining position of the weaker groups involved in the process (54); decentralisation of decision making may also help. Thus popular participation and decentralisation of economic and political power are both needed to give the rural poor better access to the food system.

NOTES AND REFERENCES

1. See, for example, W.W. Murdoch, The Poverty of Nations, Johns Hopkins University Press, Baltimore, 1980; F.M. Lappe and J. Collins, Food First: Beyond the Myth of Scarcity, Houghton Mifflin, Boston, 1977; S. George, Les stratèges de la faim, Editions Grounauer, Geneva, 1981.

2. See Sophie Bessis, L'arme Alimentaire, Maspéro, Paris, 1979, pp. 17-35.

3. Attitudes of producers are a different matter, although at times very important for export crop development. This local perception of potential profit stimulated the expansion of export crops such as cocoa in Ghana and groundnuts in Northern Nigeria.

4. See A. Sawadogo, L'agriculture en Côte d'Ivoire, Presses Universitaires de France, Paris, 1977, Chapters 14 and 22.

5. See, for example, G. Spittler, "The Transition from Subsistence Production to Market Oriented Production Among the Haussa (Niger)", in Vierteljahresberichte, No. 79, 1980, pp. 47-55.

6. See A. Sawadogo, op. cit., p. 65.

7. The general unreliability of data has recently been stressed by U. Lele and W. Candler, "Food Security: Some East African Considerations", in A. Valdes (ed.), Food Security for Developing Countries, Westview Press, Boulder, Colorado, 1981; see also J. Klatzman, "Besoins alimentaires et potentialités des pays en voie de développement", in Mondes en Développement, No. 29-30, 1980.

8. Mainly developing countries in Oceania.

9. It should be noted that the available food production index (as calculated by FAO) does not permit a distinction to be made between production for domestic consumption and production for exports, nor between products for human consumption and for animal feeding.

10. Increased food imports, as shown in Chapter III, reflect the inadequacy of domestic production.

11. FAO, "Agriculture: Towards 2000", C79/24, July 1979, p. XXV; this report is a preliminary version of a publication with the same title to which reference will be made henceforth as FAO, AT 2000 (1981). Since the earlier version provides more detailed data on certain points than the final publication, the latter cannot always be substituted for the former.

12. For a recent survey of some of the issues regarding export croping versus food self-sufficiency see J.S. Hillman, "The Role of Export Cropping in Less Developed Countries", in American Journal of Agricultural Economics, Vol. 63, No. 2, May 1981.

13. See, for example, J. Berthelot and F. de Ravignan, Les sillons de la faim, textes rassemblés par le Groupe de la Déclaration de Rome, L'Harmattan, Paris, 1980, for the case of banana production and exports in the Dominican Republic.

14. See, for example, S. George, op. cit.

15. Note that the list of countries has been drawn up to show the extremes.

16. See L. Rabello de Castro, "Brazil's Farm Conflict", in South, July 1981.

17. See FAO, Production Yearbook, Vol. 35, 1981.

18. See FAO, Production Yearbook.

19. The concentration of the best land on export crops is reported by M. Labonne and A. Hibon, Futur agricole et alimentaire de la Méditerranée arabe, INRA, December 1978, p. 52.

20. See, for example, the experience of some areas of Mexico.

21. L.R. Brown, The 29th Day, W.W. Norton, New York, 1978, p. 156.

22. See, for example, Hugues Dupriez, Paysans d'Afrique Noire, ed. Terres et Vie, Nivelles (Belgium), 1980.

23. For more details and for priorities in agricultural research see Kenneth R.M. Anthony et al., Agriculture Change in Tropical Africa, Cornell University Press, Ithaca, 1979.

24. Ibid., p. 242, gives the Kenya Tea Development Authority as an example.

25. Sophie Bessis, op. cit., pp. 40-44.

26. Statistisches Bundesamt, Feldstudie Ägypten, Vol. 5, Wiesbaden, 1976.

27. See H. Dupriez, op. cit., pp. 153-154.

28. See A. Sawadogo, op. cit., pp. 80-83.

29. For a balanced review see G. Arroyo, "Agriculture and Multinational Corporations in Latin America", in V. Harle (ed.), The Political Economy of Food, Saxon House, Westmead, 1978, and G. Ghersi et al., Multinational Firms and Agro-Food Systems in Developing Countries -- A Bibliographic Review, OECD Development Centre, Paris, 1981.

30. See M. Anson-Meyer, "Activités d'exportation de produits primaires et développement économique", in Mondes en Développement, No. 29-30, 1980.

31. See R. Goldberg, "The Role of the Multinational Corporation", in American Journal of Agricultural Economics, Vol. 63, No. 2, May 1981 and the discussion by T. Ozawa in the same volume.

32. See. G. Arroyo, op. cit.

33. For a recent review of agricultural supply elasticities in 27 countries, see Willis L. Peterson, "International Farm Prices and the Social Cost of Cheap Food Policies", in American Journal of Agricultural Economics, Vol. 61, No. 1, February 1979, pp. 12-21.

34. See M. Anson-Meyer, op.cit.

35. P. Oesterdiekhoff, K. Wohlmuth, "Handlungsspielräume des Unterentwickelten Agrarlandes Sudan", in Diskurs, (University Bremen) No. 3, August 1980.

36. For Sudan, see P. Oesterdiekhoff, "Neue Weltwirtschaftsordnung und Kleinbäuerliche Exportproduktion in LLDCs", in Diskurs, No. 3, August 1980.

37. M. Anson-Meyer, op. cit.

38. See P. Oesterdiekhoff, op. cit., p.187.

39. See A. Sawadogo, op. cit., p. 137.

40. Export crop development may have other social implications, of course, such as the disruption of family life and tradition, but they also apply to many other development efforts.

41. See S. George, op. cit., p. 129 for an example from Senegal; similarly, for Togo, see M. Anson-Meyer, op. cit., p. 189, and for Brazil, see L. Rabello de Castro, op. cit., p. 34.

42. See J. Berthelot and F. de Ravignan, op. cit., p. 137, with reference to cassava growers in Thailand.

43. G. Arroyo, op. cit., p. 203.

44. W.W. Murdoch, op. cit., p. 233; the modern sector may produce goods for direct consumption by the "elite" or procure the foreign exchange needed for imports consumed by the "elite".

45. See A. Sawadogo, op. cit., p. 67.

46. See S. Bedrani, "Algérie: la dépendance alimentaire s'accroit", in Afrique Agriculture, June 1981, pp. 20-46.

47. See also D.G. Sisler and D. Blandford, Rubber or Rice? -- The Dilemma of Many Developing Nations, World Food Issues Series, Centre for the Analysis of World Food Issues, Cornell University, Ithaca, 1979.

48. See the interview with the Ivorian Minister of Agriculture in Afrique Agriculture, No. 67, March 1981.

49. See FAO, "Examen et analyse de la réforme agraire et du développement rural dans les pays en voie de développement depuis le milieu des années soixante", CMRADR/INF.3, Rome, 1979, p. 115.

50. See R. Taton, "Agro-industries alimentaires et cultures vivrières", in Europe Outremer, no. 610, November 1980.

51. See A. Gassou, "Un Togo prospère, fier et autosuffisant", in Afrique Agriculture, No. 72, August 1981.

52. See P. Oesterdiekhoff, op. cit., p. 188.

53. See D. Morgan, The Merchants of Grain, Viking Press, New York, 1979.

54. See also G. Arroyo, op. cit., p. 213.

Chapter III

IMPORTS AND THE DOMESTIC FOOD CHAIN

INTRODUCTION

The pattern of food trade has changed radically over the last few decades. Developing countries as a group became food importers after World War II (whereas they were net exporters before) and their reliance on food imports has been growing steadily (see Table 5) (1). Imports have grown not only in absolute terms, as shown in Table 6, but, with the exception of the Far East, also as a proportion of production in the developing regions. The relative growth of cereals imports is most striking in the case of Africa. Despite increasing imports, however, food needs are not covered adequately. An estimate in a recent FAO study (2) puts the number of seriously under-nourished people at an average 435 million for 1974-1976.

It seems unlikely that developing countries as a group will become self-sufficient in cereals (3) over the next two decades, but for some individual countries there is scope for improvement. Without prejudging the issue of what degree of food self-sufficiency would be desirable for a country, it is helpful for policy formulation to examine systematically how food imports can affect (and have actually affected) the food system.

Attempts to explain and project the level of food imports take growth of population and income as their major independent variables. We shall not replicate such projections but complement them by asking what role imports play in various countries and groups of countries, and how the several components of the food system are affected by food imports.

The underlying causal relationships are not always easy to identify; in any event they do not all work in the same direction. The level of food imports is influenced by the overall development strategy adopted (e.g. emphasis on heavy industrialisation and neglect of domestic food production) but the development strategy is itself conditioned by the level of food imports. Thus, while an industrialisation strategy may require food imports, the latter may affect the pattern of industrialisation, since food imports may pre-empt a good part of the import capability of the country, leaving little for investment in industry.

An important question is, of course, how the consumers are affected by food imports. Again the answer is not easy to find. The immediate positive

Table 5

CHANGING PATTERN OF WORLD GRAIN TRADE: 1934-1981
(Million tonnes)
(Export +; Import -)

Region	1934-38	1948-52	1960	1970	1976	1981 (1)
North America	+5	+23	+39	+56	+94	+135
Latin America	+9	+1	0	+4	-3	-4
Western Europe	-24	-22	-25	-30	-17	-4
Eastern Europe and USSR	+5	0	0	+1	-25	-53
Africa	+1	0	-2	-5	-10	-16
Asia	+2	-6	-17	-37	-47	-65
Australia and New Zealand	+3	+3	+6	+12	+8	+13

1.   From FAO Trade Yearbook, Vol. 35, 1981.

Source: L. Brown, The 29th Day: Accommodating Human Needs and Numbers to the Earth's Resources, W.W. Norton, New York, 1978.

N.B.:   For 1982/83 cereals imports of developing countries are estimated at 104 million t, see FAO Food Outlook, No. 3, 1983.

effects of low-priced imported food may be replaced by the hardships of high-priced food in the future, if there is an upward trend in world market prices or concessional food supplies are discontinued. In the meantime, the opportunities for increased domestic production and increased productivity may have been foregone because of the depressing effects of (temporary) cheap food imports. Furthermore, consumers are not a homogeneous groups; they do not have equal access to imported and domestically produced food. Finally, imported food may offer the consumer a greater choice, but he may or may not be aware of and take into account its nutritional quality.

Food imports are sometimes seen to be part of a self-reinforcing "vicious circle of under-development". Thus, the satisfaction of increased urban food needs through imports may depress domestic agriculture; this in turn leads to further urbanisation via rural-urban migration and to a further increase in food imports and external debt. The only way, it seems, for developing countries to break out of such a vicious circles is to strengthen their own domestic agriculture. This may require the import of inputs.

Table 6

RELATIVE IMPORTANCE OF CEREAL IMPORTS BY DEVELOPING REGIONS (1)

(annual average in 1000 tonnes)

		Africa	Latin America	Near East	Far East
(1)	**Production**				
	1961-1963	35 940	49 724	36 099	169 302
	1970-1972	43 579	70 264	44 452	215 816
	1977-1979	44 910	85 372	53 385	257 940
	1979-1981	46 019	92 722	56 028	272 310
(2)	**Imports**				
	1961-1963	2 954	5 778	4 865	11 516
	1970-1972	4 939	8 422	7 361	13 955
	1977-1979	10 423	16 847	15 473	15 510
	1979-1981	14 054	22 469	20 120	17 641
(3)	**Imports in % of Production**				
	1961-1963	8.2	11.6	13.0	6.8
	1970-1972	11.3	12.0	16.6	6.5
	1977-1979	23.2	19.7	29.0	6.0
	1979-1981	30.5	24.2	35.9	6.5

1.　　Developing market economies only;　figures exclude intra-regional trade.

Source:　FAO Production Yearbooks and Trade Yearbooks, various editions.

1. THE ROLE OF MAJOR IMPORTED INPUTS

The spectacular increase in food production known as the "Green Revolution", which had its first decade from 1965 to 1975, depended heavily on imported inputs such as seeds, fertilizers, pesticides and equipment for irrigation. There are no easy options: if this production model is to be followed, many developing countries will have to increase their imports of inputs considerably or follow import substitution policies. While "hopeful equations for agricultural production based on cheap, plentiful energy inputs may have to be rewritten" (4) the general view seems to be that substantial increases in investment and inputs will be required to prevent massive food deficits in low-income countries.

Increased availability of modern inputs is a necessary but not sufficient condition to effectively achieve growth in output. For this to happen, inputs have to be technically mastered and efficiently used. Algeria provides an example where this has not yet been the case; agricultural production has stagnated despite increasing imports of inputs, perhaps because of weaknesses in the delivery system or insufficient research, or both.

In a study of 16 "rapid-growth" countries, it has also been found that the link between inputs and yield has not always been clear: "Although overall increases in fertilizer use and irrigation were closely associated with yield increases of staple food crops in many countries, the association was poor in some countries" (5).

Another critical point for the effective use of modern inputs is the new element of risk faced by producers. It is of a dual nature. First, there is the risk that the input will not have the expected output effect if one or more elements of the "package" are missing, including those on which the producer may have no influence, such as rainfall. Second, there is the risk that increased production will not meet with an adequate output delivery system and remunerative prices. Only if these risks can be minimised (for example by irrigation, drought resistant seeds and marketing arrangements) in relation to producers' capacity to take risks, will imported inputs be effectively used.

a) Fertilizers

Three principal types of fertilizer have to be considered, viz. those based on nitrogen, phosphate and potash. The industrial countries of the North have been and still are the major producers and consumers of all types of fertilizers. But since the raw materials of nitrogen fertilizers (fossil fuels) and of phosphate fertilizers (phosphate rock) are also available in certain developing countries, the list of producers now includes an increasing number of these countries. The 20 major producer countries of nitrogen fertilizers accounted for over 86 per cent of world production in 1967-1968 but for only 66 per cent in 1980-1981. In this group, India and Egypt are the only developing countries, but it is remarkable that India now ranks third behind the United States and the USSR, whereas ten years ago it was number 12 (for details see Tables 7 and 8).

While the relative increase in fertilizer consumption has been much higher over the last decade in developing countries than in the developed countries, the consumption level in the latter is still more than three times that of the former (113 kg/ha as against 34 kg/ha). However, there are large variations between countries and regions. Consumption is lowest in Africa, between 5 and 10 per cent of the level of developed countries.

Morocco holds the biggest share in world exports of phosphate rock (33 per cent in 1977-1978) but counts for only a small share in exports of phosphate fertilizers (2 per cent in 1977-1978), which are dominated by the United States (55 per cent). India, South Korea, Turkey, Cuba, Chile and Colombia ranked highest among developing countries as importers of phosphate fertilizers in 1967-1968. A decade later, all but Turkey had decreased and even (Korea) discontinued imports of phosphate fertilizers.

Table 7

FERTILIZER PRODUCTION BY REGION IN 1967/68 AND 1980/81

(in 1 000 tonnes and as a percentage of world production)

Region	Nitrogen		Phosphate		Potash		Total	
	1967/68	1980/81	1967/68	1980/81	1967/68	1980/81	1967/68	1980/81
DEVELOPED COUNTRIES								
Market Economies	17 048 (66.6)	26 888 (42.9)	13 170 (73.1)	18 165 (52.7)	10 145 (66.3)	15 903 (58.0)	40 445 (67.2)	60 957 (48.9)
Centrally Planned Economies	5 843 (22.8)	16 283 (26.0)	3 229 (17.9)	8 741 (25.4)	5 073 (33.2)	11 486 (41.9)	15 053 (25.0)	36 508 (29.3)
Total Developed Countries	22 891 (87.4)	43 171 (68.9)	16 399 (91.0)	26 906 (78.1)	15 218 (99.5)	27 389 (99.8)	55 498 (92.2)	97 465 (78.2)
DEVELOPING COUNTRIES								
Africa	3 (0.1)	221 (0.4)	399 (1.9)	707 (2.1)	-	-	345 (0.6)	929 (0.7)
Latin America	511 (2.0)	1 719 (2.7)	239 (1.3)	1 919 (5.6)	18 (0.1)	23 (0.1)	993 (1.7)	3 663 (2.9)
Near East	267 (1.0)	2 006 (3.2)	101 (0.6)	594 (1.7)	-	-	369 (0.6)	2 600 (2.1)
Far East	772 (3.0)	4 704 (7.5)	284 (1.6)	1 730 (5.0)	-	-	994 (1.7)	6 434 (5.2)
Total Market Economy	1 555 (6.1)	8 650 (13.8)	964 (5.3)	4 950 (14.4)	18 (0.1)	23 (0.1)	2 703 (4.5)	13 626 (10.9)
Asian Centrally Planned Economy	1 143 (4.5)	10 878 (17.3)	660 (3.7)	2 550 (7.4)	55 (0.4)	20 (0.1)	1 969 (3.3)	13 450 (10.8)
Total Developing Countries	2 698 (10.6)	19 530 (31.1)	1 624 (9.0)	7 537 (21.9)	73 (0.5)	43 (0.2)	4 672 (7.8)	27 111 (21.8)
TOTAL WORLD	25 590	62 700	18 024	34 443	15 291	27 432	60 170	124 577

Source: FAO Annual Fertilizer Review, 1972; FAO Fertilizer Yearbook, 1978.

Table 8

MAIN PRODUCER COUNTRIES OF NITROGEN FERTILIZERS AND THEIR SHARE OF
WORLD NITROGEN FERTILIZER PRODUCTION IN 1967/68 and 1980/81

| | 1967/1968 | | 1980/1981 | |
	1000 MT	%	1000 MT	%
United States	6 607	25.8	11 788	18.8
Soviet Union	3 753	14.7	10 155	16.2
Japan	2 034	8.0	1 202	2.0
Fed. Rep. of Germany	1 559	6.1	1 436	2.3
France	1 239	4.8	1 690	2.6
Italy	1 095	4.3	1 387	2.2
United Kingdom	855	3.3	1 167	1.9
Netherlands	849	3.3	1 623	2.6
Poland	593	2.3	1 290	2.0
Canada	470	1.8	1 755	2.8
Spain	424	1.7	959	1.5
Belgium	402	1.6	743	1.2
India	402	1.6	2 163	3.4
Norway	358	1.4	427	0.7
Bulgaria	353	1.4	730	1.2
Dem. Rep. of Germany	336	1.3	943	1.5
Austria	252	1.0	300	0.5
Czechoslovakia	245	1.0	735	1.2
Hungary	184	0.7	651	1.0
Egypt	146	0.6	400	0.6
Others	3 426	13.4	21 206	33.8
World Total	25 590		62 700	

Source: FAO, Annual Fertilizer Review, various editions.

As to potash fertilizers, developed countries are practically the only
producers (over 98 per cent in 1977-1978). Major developing country importers
were Brazil and India, covering 60-70 per cent of their consumption through
imports.

The location of productive capacities and reserves makes developing
countries import-dependent, but there is a tendency and further scope for
import substitution in many of the more important consumer countries. However, in certain cases this may simply shift the dependence from the finished
product to the raw material and feedstock.

The way in which import substitution in fertilizers will affect food
production depends mainly on pricing and distribution practices. Fertilizer
demand is relatively price elastic. If governments would allow fertilizers to

be imported without any duty, it would, in most cases, be difficult for domestic producers to compete with the imports from industrialised countries with regard to prices. The main reasons are economies of scale and continuous high rates of capacity use in the latter which cannot be achieved in developing countries, at least at an initial stage of industrialisation. To promote agriculture, and sometimes also to support the buiding-up of a domestic fertilizer industry, many governments subsidise fertilizer prices in one way or another. But the extent to which this benefits food crops depends on the distribution and actual use of fertilizers.

High internal transport costs, uncertain timing of the supply, weak extension services and limited availability of credit are often among the obstacles to be overcome for an effective and general use of fertilizers for food crops, even if relative prices make fertilizer use an economic proposition. Governments therefore often feel that they have to play an active role in integrating the different components of the fertilizer distribution system.

Egypt is a good example of a highly centralised consumer-oriented distribution system where the Agricultural Credit Organisation (ACO) has exclusive rights to the procurement and wholesaling of fertilizers. All local fertilizer factories are obliged to sell their production through this Organisation, which also buys all imports from government importing companies. The centralised national supply is then sold by ACO to the farmers' co-operatives which retail fertilizers in every village. The ACO also has warehouses and its own retail outlets from which farmers can obtain their fertilizer requirements.

Thus, the impact of modern inputs on food crop production depends not so much, if at all, on the origin of the input (foreign or domestic) but on the terms and conditions under which it is effectively available and used by producers. In addition to physical availability at the right time and appropriate quality, the relation between input and output prices is of paramount importance.

b) Pesticides

The importance of pesticides is obvious in view of the fact that approximately one-third of the world's potential agricultural production is lost due to pests, insects and plant diseases (6). Furthermore, pest problems are often intensified as yields are increased through plant breeding and increased irrigation.

As with fertilizers, production and consumption of pesticides are concentrated in developed countries. Developing regions are the only major net importers (see Table 9). Among the few developing countries which manufacture basic toxicants and finished formulations with little or no imports of raw materials are Argentina, Peru, Kenya, Rwanda, Tanzania, India and Pakistan. The relatively small and uncertain market for pesticides in developing countries has not provided incentives to industry to develop new pesticides specifically for the different crops and local conditions in these countries. But organisations such as the International Rice Research Institute, the FAO Pesticide Laboratories and others are testing new compounds and making recommendations concerning more appropriate pesticide products for developing regions.

Table 9

INTERNATIONAL TRADE IN PESTICIDES BY REGIONS
IN 1971 and 1980 (in million US $)

	1971			1980		
	Imports	Exports	Balance	Imports	Exports	Balance
North America	44	118	74	448	569	121
Western Europe	214	464	250	1 666	2 888	1 222
Oceania	9	4	-5	33	10	-23
Other developed countries	41	38	-3	180	202	22
Total developed market economies	308	624	316	2 327	3 669	1 342
Africa	55	5	-50	309	32	-277
Latin America	105	10	-95	387	104	-283
Near East	58	2	-56	288	6	-282
Far East	64	6	-58	272	79	-193
Other developing countries	2	-	-2	10	-	-10
Total developing market economies	285	23	-262	1 256	221	-1 035

Source: FAO Trade Yearbook Vols. 31 and 35.

Major constraints for higher levels of pesticide use in developing countries are the high cost and the absence of an appropriate research/extension/distribution system. An ecologically sound and economically interesting way of loosening such constraints consists in the development and implementation of "integrated pest control", incorporating the use of both natural defense mechanisms (crop rotation, predators, viruses and other biological means) and chemical agents.

c) Tractors

The range of agricultural equipment and machinery imported by developing countries is too wide to be covered here. Since tractors constitute a central and often symbolic element in farm mechanisation and since data on tractor trade are more easily available (7), this is the only category of agricultural machinery included in this brief review.

In 1978, developing market economies imported 174 000 tractors. This represented approximately 22 per cent of world tractor imports in terms of quantity and nearly 33 per cent in value terms. This suggests an excessive share of expensive (powerful and sophisticated) tractors in developing countries' imports and possibly also above-average shipping costs (since import value is reported c.i.f.). Although the higher value proportion may be partly explained by the inclusion of heavy earth-movers in the tractor trade statistics, the question of the appropriateness of the imported tractors has to be posed. The answer can only be based on the analysis of a specific country situation (8). But it is interesting to note that in one survey, all major manufacturers commented negatively on the current discussions about producing a small inexpensive tractor for the needs of developing countries. The general argument was that the basic tractor now available could not be simplified without making it ineffective in most developing country conditions. Further, manufacturers who have produced a special, very simple model found that there was not sufficient interest in it in developing countries since these countries tend to demand the most technically advanced, comfortable machines (9).

There are situations, of course, where tractors, combined with other inputs, may be indispensable for a rapid increase in food production. This can be the case where multiple cropping is introduced and a very short time span is available to carry out crucial cultivation tasks. This intensification of production can also be a way of reconciling conflicts between food crops and export crops by increasing the productivity of the land and thus satisfying both increasing food needs and growing foreign exchange requirements. However, as in the case of other inputs, importing the necessary equipment alone is not sufficient to achieve the desired results. Its use and maintenance require local structures and resources (manpower and finance) to be geared to the efficient operation of the equipment. Furthermore, high energy prices and environmental stress may suggest a reconsideration of the need and intensity of tractor use which may have been justified by conditions which no longer exist.

Policy Implications

If the technical appropriateness of specific inputs is ascertained in a given country (including the existence and functioning of the necessary support structure) and if their domestic production is not feasible, either technically or economically, importing would seem justified if the use of these inputs is economically profitable. A corollary of government involvement in production support systems (e.g. research and extension) and the tight foreign exchange situation in many developing countries is that public institutions usually play an important role in determining what is being imported and under what conditions. Care has to be taken to ensure the procurement of imports on the most favourable economic terms. Even if it is maintained that the world market for agricultural inputs is basically a competitive market, the size of the market of many developing countries is too small to accommodate several suppliers on a permanent basis. After an initial bidding phase, competition may be severely restricted or nonexistent within the country, in which case the public authorities will have to take measures (e.g. contractual arrangements, market surveillance) to prevent the abuse of oligopolistic or monopolistic positions by foreign suppliers or importers.

However, governments have sometimes increased the cost of inputs to domestic users by charging import taxes or by banning imports in order to protect domestic industries. This may discourage the use of the inputs concerned and can thus be self-defeating, i.e. provide neither the expected fiscal income nor the market for the domestically-produced goods. Domestic production and use of inputs may therefore have to be subsidised. Thus government intervention at one point in the system may trigger off a series of other interventions. Policy measures concerning inputs therefore have to be based on an analysis of the whole system and of the costs and benefits not only in the short, but also in the longer term.

2. PATTERNS OF FOOD IMPORTS

The picture of change in the regional import pattern presented in Tables 5 and 6 needs to be complemented in several ways. First, the groups of countries shown are not homogeneous and obviously do not constitute integrated political units capable of designing and implementing policies based on the diagnosis of their food situation as a group. Therefore, the analysis has to descend to the national level. Moreover, a further differentiation is necessary to take into account disparities between groups within countries.

The regrouping of countries by income level rather than regional location provides some indications of the trends in food imports, as demonstrated for cereals in Table 10. From 1970 to 1981, middle-income countries increased their imports by more than 200 per cent, bringing their share in world imports from 21 per cent to 28.9 per cent, while the share of all developing countries' imports grew from 40 to only 43 per cent. Looking at individual middle-income countries, several have become important only in the last decade, and some major importers such as Brazil, Mexico, Korea and Egypt have multiplied their cereal imports by factors ranging from three to seven during that period.

In the group of major low-income importers, the contrast between China and India is particularly noteworthy. While India's annual cereal imports have fallen from 4 to 1.5 million tons over the period 1970-1981, those of China grew from 6 to 17 million tons. Thus, the declining share of low-income countries (from 16 to 11.6 per cent of world imports) does not reflect a general trend within this group of countries but is the result of a complex pattern of change.

In Table 10, no sub-Saharan African countries have been singled out, because individually they are not among the major importers. However, cereal imports compared to domestic production have grown most vigorously in Africa over the last two decades, nearly quadrupling from 8.2 per cent in 1961-63 to 30.5 per cent in 1979-1981 (see Table 6). This share is second only to that of the Near East (35.9 per cent), which includes more countries with a strong financial capacity to sustain food imports: it is in sharp contrast to the situation in the Far East where the proportion fell from 6.8 per cent to 6.5 per cent over the same period.

It would be a mistake, however, to conclude that, thanks to the strong growth of cereal imports in Africa, all food requirements have been met. The situation varies greatly among African countries.

Table 10

CEREAL IMPORTS BY MAJOR DEVELOPING COUNTRY IMPORTERS
(million tonnes)

	1970		1981				
	TOTAL CEREALS tonnes	SHARE %	TOTAL CEREALS tonnes	SHARE %	WHEAT tonnes	COARSE GRAINS tonnes	RICE tonnes
World Imports	103	100	232	100	104	114.4	13.6
Developing countries Total	41	40	100	43	60	29.8	10.2
-- LOW INCOME	16	16	27	11.6	19	6.4	1.6
Bangladesh	2	2	1	0.4	1.0	--	--
China	6	6	17	7.3	13.0	3.8	0.2
Cuba	1	1	2	0.9	1.2	0.6	0.2
India	4	4	1.5	0.6	1.4	0.1	--
Low income less China/India	6	6	5.5	2.4	4.6	--	1.4
-- MIDDLE INCOME	22	21	67	28.9	35	25.5	6.5
-- Low Middle Income	9	9	21	9.1	14	5.2	1.8
Egypt	1	1	7	3.0	6	1.0	--
Indonesia	1	1	2	0.9	1.4	0.1	0.5
Morocco	--	--	3	1.3	2.4	0.6	--
-- High Middle Income	12	12	46	19.8	21	20.3	4.7
Algeria	--	--	3	1.3	2.7	0.3	--
Brazil	2	2	6	2.6	4.4	1.5	0.1
Korea	2	2	8	3.4	1.9	3.5	2.6
Iran	--	--	3	1.3	2.0	0.5	0.5
Iraq	--	--	2	0.9	1.6	--	0.4
Mexico	1	1	7	3.0	1.0	5.9	0.4
Venezuela	1	1	2	0.9	0.9	1.1	0.1
-- HIGH INCOME	3	3	6	2.6	6	--	2.1
Saudi Arabia	1	1	4	1.7	1	2.6	0.4

--   Signifies less than 0.1 million tonnes.

Source: FAO Trade Yearbook 1973 and 1981.

60

If one distinguishes low-income countries and middle-income countries in sub-Saharan Africa, the cereal imports pattern shown earlier in Table 10 for all developing countries is only partly confirmed (see Table 11). First, cereal imports (commercial and non-commercial flows) of middle-income oil-importing countries grew even more rapidly (120 per cent in four years) than in all middle-income developing countries. Second, and different from the group of all low-income countries, the sub-Saharan low-income countries were still the main cereal importers in the region in 1979. But if one considers only commercial cereal imports, the middle-income oil-importing countries dominate with regard to both the absolute level and the growth of cereal imports. On a per capita basis, their total net cereals inflow nearly doubled from 1975 to 1979, whereas that of the low-income countries declined slightly.

Table 11

CEREAL IMPORTS OF SELECTED GROUPS OF AFRICAN COUNTRIES

	1975	1976	1977	1978	1979
Total net cereals inflow (unit: 1 000 tonnes)					
Low-income countries	2 306.5	1 958.2	2 241.1	2 489.7	2 225.0
Middle-income oil-importing countries	760.1	877.9	1 471.7	1 726.8	1 673.7
Total Africa	3 776.1	3 802.5	5 081.2	6 106.4	5 484.1
Commercial net cereals imports (unit: 1 000 tonnes)					
Low-income countries	1 471.8	1 309.7	1 532.9	1 488.7	1 272.0
Middle-income oil-importing countries	646.9	779.5	1 324.0	1 389.9	1 439.1
Total Africa	2 818.3	3 050.5	4 212.6	4 747.2	4 282.6
Total net cereals inflow per capita (kilograms)					
Low-income countries	13.6	11.3	12.6	13.6	11.8
Middle-income oil-importing countries	14.6	16.4	26.6	30.2	28.3
Total Africa	12.4	12.2	15.8	18.5	16.2

Source: The World Bank, Accelerated Development in Sub-Saharan Africa, 1981, p.49, Washington, D.C., based on Food Aid Bulletin, No.4, FAO, Rome, 1980.

Considerable variations in the cereal import and supply situation within a single ecological zone such as the Sahel can be seen from Tables 12 and 13. While all Sahel countries have increasingly relied on cereal imports over the last two decades, the volume has not always been sufficient to fully make up for the shortfalls of domestic supply. Three patterns of import dependence can be distinguished for these countries (see Table 12). In the first group of countries, imports had to make up for declining domestic production in addition to meeting growing demand due to population and income growth. Mauritania and Gambia belong to this category which is characterised by falling rates of self-sufficiency (except for the latest years). In a second group of countries (Upper Volta, Mali, Niger), cereal imports increased despite some growth of domestic production. Even in years of production shortfalls in these countries, the self-sufficiency rate remained at a high level (mostly over 95 per cent) because imports were not increased to compensate for the shortfall. In fact, overall supply fluctuated greatly. Third, Senegal may be considered to be in a category of its own, with self-sufficiency rates oscillating around 65 per cent. However, in this country too, import levels are not geared to production shortfalls but are maintained at a relatively stable and high level, since domestic production fluctuates.

Over the last two decades cereal production per person has declined in all the Sahel countries listed in Table 13, though Upper Volta, Niger and Senegal show a less drastic reduction than the other countries. While imports per person generally increased over the period under consideration (with Niger switching from being an exporter to an importer), these increases have not been high enough to compensate for the production decline on a per capita basis.

Although the general pattern holds for all Sahel countries, there are considerable differences in their per capita level of cereal imports. It is striking that the country with the highest per capita imports (Mauritania) also shows the lowest per capita supply during the second half of the 1970s. By contrast, the two other countries with relatively high levels of cereal imports per capita (Senegal and Gambia) are also among those with the highest per capita supply, and the country with the highest average per capita supply (Niger) has been only a marginal importer. In other words, while imports have complemented domestic production in all countries, they have not been commensurate with production shortfalls.

3. THE BURDEN OF FOOD IMPORTS IN PERSPECTIVE

Growing levels of cereal imports in developing countries have given rise to preoccupation about these countries' continued capacity to finance them. However, a comparison of the shares of food imports in total merchandise imports for the years 1960 and 1978 for 54 LDCs for which data is available (10) shows that, on average, these shares decreased from 22 to 17 per cent for low-income countries and from 15 to 12 per cent for middle-income countries. While for most countries the shares declined, they remained high and food imports do indeed constitute a heavy burden on the economies of the poor countries. Only in two low-income countries (the Central African Republic and Sudan) did the shares of food imports increase. By contrast, among the middle-income countries, the statistics for Mexico show a most spectacular increase from 4 to 13 per cent.

Table 12

TOTAL CEREAL SUPPLY IN MAJOR SAHEL COUNTRIES
(unit: 1 000 tonnes)

	1961-65	1968	1971	1973	1975	1976	1977	1978	1979	1980	1981
Gambia											
Production	86	88	88	80	94	68	48	71	57	80	91
Exports											
Imports	11	16	12	17	15	50	35	61	45	47	48
Supply	97	104	100	97	109	118	83	132	102	127	139
Self-sufficiency (%)	88.7	84.6	88.0	82.5	86.2	57.6	57.8	53.8	55.9	63.0	65.5
Upper Volta											
Production	918	1 084	881	843	1 257	1 194	1 055	1 208	1 212	1 036	1 299
Exports											
Imports	14	18	19	39	21	24	54	63	81	84	71
Supply	932	1 102	900	882	1 278	1 218	1 109	1 271	1 293	1 120	1 370
Self-sufficiency (%)	98.5	98.4	97.9	95.6	98.4	98.0	95.1	95.0	93.7	92.5	94.8
Mali											
Production	1 055	963	1 154	709	1 012	1 229	1 070	1 419	1 236	955	1 204
Exports							8				
Imports	9	10	63	156	120	56		69	40	90	102
Supply	1 064	973	1 217	865	1 132	1 285	1 062	1 488	1 276	1 045	1 306
Self-sufficiency (%)	99.2	99.0	94.8	82.0	89.4	95.6	100.8	95.4	96.8	91.4	92.2
Mauritania											
Production	98	55	80	34	38	38	29	26	44	29	80
Exports											
Imports	38	60	75	105	99	125	148	150	87	162	182
Supply	136	115	115	139	137	163	177	176	131	191	262
Self-sufficiency (%)	72.1	47.8	51.6	24.5	27.7	23.3	16.4	14.8	33.6	15.2	30.5
Niger											
Production	1 218	922	880	803	871	1 347	1 508	1 530	1 629	1 797	1 442
Exports	33	42	52	20	11				20	20	30
Imports						29	23	64	34	58	89
Supply	1 185	880	828	783	860	1 376	1 531	1 594	1 643	1 835	1 501
Self-sufficiency (%)	102.8	104.8	106.3	102.6	101.3	97.9	98.5	96.0	99.1	97.9	96.1
Chad											
Production	759	764	693	507	564	590	622	648	652	678	661
Exports											
Imports	4	5	9	20	10	19	20	18	20	8	14
Supply	763	769	702	527	574	609	642	666	672	686	675
Self-sufficiency (%)	99.5	99.3	98.7	96.2	98.3	96.9	96.9	97.3	97.0	98.8	97.9
Senegal											
Production	617	537	729	624	786	714	517	996	665	645	928
Exports											
Imports	210	242	357	444	210	333	420	400	505	414	458
Supply	827	779	1 086	1 068	996	1 047	937	1 396	1 170	1 052	1 384
Self-sufficiency (%)	74.6	68.9	67.1	58.4	78.9	68.2	55.2	71.3	56.8	61.3	67.1

Sources: FAO Production Yearbook, 1979, 1978, 1977, 1976, 1975, 1973, 1972
Food Trade Yearbook, 1979, 1977, 1975, 1973, 1972.

Table 13

CEREAL SUPPLY PER PERSON (kg/year)

	1961-65	1968	1971	1973	1975	1976	1977	1978	1979
I. Production									
Gambia	239	200	183	160	181	126	87	125	133
Upper Volta	197	209	161	146	207	192	165	184	170
Mali	231	191	215	126	167	197	167	216	154
Mauritania	94	47	63	25	27	26	19	17	28
Niger	376	243	215	185	190	285	310	307	316
Chad	238	218	186	131	140	143	148	150	146
Senegal	184	135	165	133	158	140	99	185	123
II. Foreign Trade									
Gambia	31	36	25	34	29	93	64	107	62
Upper Volta	3	4	4	7	4	4	9	10	8
Mali	2	2	12	28	20	9	-1	11	5
Mauritania	37	51	59	78	70	86	99	97	96
Niger	-10	-11	-13	-5	-2	6	5	13	5
Chad	1	1	2	5	3	5	5	4	5
Senegal	63	61	81	95	42	65	80	74	70
III. Supply									
Gambia	269	236	208	194	210	219	151	232	195
Upper Volta	200	213	164	152	211	196	174	194	179
Mali	233	193	226	154	187	206	166	227	159
Mauritania	131	98	121	103	97	112	118	114	123
Niger	366	232	202	180	187	292	315	319	322
Chad	239	220	189	137	142	148	153	155	150
Senegal	247	195	246	227	200	205	179	260	194

Source: Table 12 and UN Demographic Yearbook, Special Issue - Historical Supplement, Monthly Bulletin of Statistics, August 1981.

This change in the relative weight of food imports is, of course, linked to changes in the other major items of merchandise imports such as fuels, other raw materials, machinery and other manufactures while the situation varies between countries, the share of fuel imports has increased most strongly on average, from 6 per cent to 11 per cent for low-income countries. According to the data available (11), it affected all but the eleven oil-exporting countries. The shares of other imported items have changed in a less uniform pattern as between groups of countries and, of course, even more so as between individual countries.

In summary, then, it is correct to say that, for the period 1960-1978, and for low-income countries, food imports represented on average a heavier burden than imports of fuel, although the share of the latter increased while the share of the former declined. The situation was reversed over the same period for middle-income countries whose fuel imports reached a higher share than food imports.

Another reason for underlining the burden of food imports on many developing countries is that most of them should be able (with existing knowledge and resources) to produce more food domestically, leaving more foreign exchange for other necessities and providing a firm base for self-sustained growth and general mobilisation of domestic resources. The potential for doing so needs to be examined for individual countries and specific circumstances. There are probably cases where a reduction of food imports would not be desirable first on principles of economics (e.g. comparative advantage), as argued in a recent World Bank study (12). However, even where applicable, the impact on distribution and on risks incurred by farmers may weaken and, at the extreme, invalidate the case in favour of food imports.

4. FOOD IMPORTS AND DOMESTIC PRODUCERS

The assertion that food imports depress domestic food production is frequently advanced. It may seem plausible, given that additional supply tends to reduce prices and push marginal producers out of the market. Numerous examples can be found in the literature. However, testing the hypothesis on the basis of time series data of food imports and domestic production for a given country, one quickly gets into difficulties since it is rarely possible to obtain detailed information about prices of different crops, trade policies and production decisions concerning the same period. Statistically, increasing imports of a given crop can be either the consequence or the cause of declining domestic production of that crop. In addition, a great number of other factors may influence both imports and domestic production; and the causal relationships may change over time.

While such statistical tests cannot prove or invalidate the above assertion as a general proposition, they underline the need for caution in interpreting incomplete data (13). In the following pages we shall point out some of the factors and mechanisms described in the literature and draw on the case-study material assembled for this project.

Food imports in developing countries are of two kinds - commercial and concessional (i.e., food aid). Overall, the latter rarely amount to more than 10 per cent of the former, but in individual countries food aid supplies have at times reached proportions of up to 100 per cent of all food imports. While the effects of the two types of food imports can be similar in many cases, we shall deal first with commercial imports only (except where otherwise stated) and take up particular issues of food aid in a subsequent sub-section.

a) Price effects

Several situations can be envisaged. Theoretically, imports may be supplied to the domestic market on terms equivalent to those obtaining for domestic products, in which case the supply curve will shift to the right and an equilibrium price below that which previously prevailed will result. In practice, however, since the demand of any one importing developing country will be small compared to the world market, the total supply curve will be practically horizontal and the equilibrium price will be even lower. In any case, if market forces work freely in a textbook fashion, domestic supply will be reduced because of the fall in market price. Even though the market mechanism in reality is more complex (making allowances for quality, location, etc.), the net effect is qualitatively as described (14).

The operation of this price-depressing mechanism is generally not instantaneous and automatic but depends on the actions of government and traders, as well as consumers and producers. The government may use imports as a convenient source of fiscal income and charge import duties, thus lifting the import supply curve and somewhat reducing the pressure on domestic prices. The same instrument of import duties may also be used with a different motivation, but with similar results, namely to protect domestic producers. In this case, the rate of duties (or alternatively a quota) may be fixed in such a way as to safeguard a given level of domestic prices. Imports will then meet only that part of the demand at those prices which domestic supply does not meet, either due to an occasional shortfall in domestic production or as a consequence of growing demand. Thus, imports may be used to prevent prices from climbing above some politically acceptable level.

It is frequently argued (15) that where local currencies are overvalued, import levies are necessary to make the import price reflect at least the true cost of foreign exchange. Another purpose of import levies, which ensure relatively high urban food prices, may be to impose a certain degree of "urban austerity", with a view to helping to restore the rural economy. In a spirit of positive adjustment, receipts from import duties can be used to strengthen and stimulate domestic production, for example by investing them in related research and infrastructure. A policy along these lines is being followed in Korea with regard to cattle imports (16). Thus, judiciously-managed imports can be prevented from having a disincentive effect and can, at the same time, provide the financial basis for the promotion of domestic production.

While there are ways and means of preventing food imports from having adverse net effects on domestic producers, these possibilities are often not utilised by policy-makers. As a rule, the food import pattern is only partly determined by a country's natural resource endowment; it is as much or more a question of political choice. A low-price policy can be pursued in a selective or a generalised way. Prices of a single or a few food crops may be depressed via imports in order to make producers switch to another crop, most likely for export. The large food imports (mostly on concessional terms) in Egypt may be explained in this way. When food producers have no possibility of switching to more profitable crops, some of them migrate to urban areas and engage in non-agricultural activities. This may be the intended effect, as seems to have been the case in Korea during the 1950s when reconstruction and early industrialisation had to draw on labour from the agricultural sector. In most countries, however, migration induced by food import policies would be considered undesirable, because there would already be surplus labour in the urban areas (17).

If, in such a situation, food imports are nevertheless allowed to depress domestic producer prices, several, not necessarily mutually exclusive, explanations are possible. First, in the case of an outward-looking industrialisation strategy, it may be argued that low food prices are necessary to support industries in their infancy via low labour costs and the accumulation of an investable surplus in the urban sector. A second explanation might be that, due to budgetary difficulties, the wages of government employees have to be kept low and this would not be possible if food prices were allowed to increase. Finally, urban groups are often seen as so politically powerful, either because they are themselves in government or because they are able to put pressure on the government, that they can successfully insist on food imports being allowed.

b) Demand and marketing effects

While food imports tend to affect domestic producers most directly via prices, there are also other effects, some of them more subtle and more long-term. Even well-managed food imports which are marketed at "reasonable prices", for example in periods of drought, can have detrimental effects for domestic producers. One case is the shift of demand to crops which are not and cannot be produced in the country but for which consumers may develop a taste. The classical example is wheat and wheat products in the humid tropics. This effect will be reinforced if the imported product has, in addition, a "prestige" value, so that consumers are willing to pay even relatively high prices for it.

Another example is the destruction of traditional marketing channels which cannot always be revived if needed. In Niger, this is reported to be a consequence of food aid supplies. In a similar vein, production structures in Algeria are seen as changing under the influence of food imports and are becoming inadequate to satisfy the national demand for basic foodstuffs (18).

Among the many practical reasons for substituting imports for domestic crops, one should mention the convenience of imported foodstuffs, which makes them easier to store, transport and process. Urban food supply in Papua New Guinea (19) is a clear example. If domestic crops are expected to keep up with imports in these respects, ways and means have to be found to improve marketing and processing, without, however, overly increasing cost.

Finally, it should not be forgotten that foreign producers and traders of the imported products and their local agents have an interest in seeing imports continue. In colonial times, the interest may have been to provide a market for the products of the colonial power. Thus in the Ivory Coast, for example, after initial promotion, local vegetable production was at one stage suppressed in favour of imports (20). Today, traders have a natural interest in making full use of the infrastructure which has been geared to the import of certain products which, moreover, may be less subject to price control than domestic staples (21). Furthermore, both government and traders value the high degree of reliability of import supply as against the vagaries of domestic production.

The argument based on the convenience of imported foodstuffs for both traders and consumers applies particularly in coastal capital cities with good overseas transport connections. However, this does not mean that it should always be accepted as policy guidance. Where it reflects poor domestic transport and marketing infrastructure or weaknesses in the domestic supply system, it will generally be economically justified to seek to remove these weaknesses over time rather than perpetuating the import dependence. There may be a trade-off between short-term, low-cost food supplies for urban areas and the objective of a more balanced development relying on stronger linkages between the various sectors and regions of the national economy.

A policy offering better food supply to urban than to rural areas due to imported food can adversely affect rural people in two ways. First, agricultural producers may lose part of their traditional or potential market and thus suffer income losses which increase rural-urban income disparities. Second, as consumers, rural people may be disadvantaged in terms of price, quality and reliability of food supplies. If, as a result, people migrate to urban areas, they will increase the pressure for food imports and thus reinforce the vicious circles which caused their own migration to the towns in the first place.

c) Differentiation among producers

So far, we have treated agricultural producers as if they were a homogeneous group. In the context of this analysis, they in fact need to be differentiated by degree of market orientation, crops produced, location and resource endowment.

Obviously, subsistence farmers, who usually produce exclusively for their own consumption, are not directly affected by food imports since, by definition, they do not participate in the market. However, in certain cases, such as food-for-work projects in a period of production shortfall, they may receive imported food. If, as a consequence, they neglect their own food production or subsequently leave their land for town (22), this category of producers is also exposed to the impact of food imports.

Other things being equal, the degree of market orientation determines the vulnerability of producers vis-a-vis food imports. If food imports are allowed to depress the prices of domestically-produced food, the income effect on producers will be proportionate to their share of market production. Bigger farmers will tend to be more affected than smaller farmers. However, where the ceteris paribus clause does not apply, the effect may be distributed differently, in particular when a time dimension is introduced. First, among producers with different levels and structures of production costs (labour, loans, inputs, rent), those with the highest costs and little scope to reduce them may be squeezed more than their market orientation would suggest. Second, those less well-placed on the market, either geographically or in terms of market implantation, may also suffer more than their degree of market orientation would imply. Finally, if one looks ahead to subsequent production periods, producers who have the necessary resources to switch to other crops (i.e., land of appropriate quality, knowledge and finance) may be able to adjust to food imports without income losses in the longer run. The different positions of producers on the market and their capacity to adjust therefore have to be considered in detail before food import policies are designed and implemented.

d) Food aid imports and domestic producers

In principle, food aid imports may affect domestic food producers in the same way as food imports on commercial terms, in particular where domestic prices are higher than import prices. However, perhaps because most of the food aid is supplied in the form of grants (approximately 75 per cent), much more attention has been paid to the potential depressing effects on domestic agriculture from food aid than from commercial food imports. There is considerable literature examining the impact in individual countries. In the 1960s and early 1970s, India and other Asian countries were studied most intensively; more recently, a number of studies have been conducted on the experience of African countries (23).

While it is very difficult to quantify the negative production effects of food aid supplies, they have been estimated for a number of countries. It seems that some of these estimates overstated the negative production effects in India for the period 1956-1962, while others (for the same country) concluded that the production effects were negligible or non-existent (24). In any case, the potential disincentive effect can be analytically reduced to three modes of influence. First, pressure on market prices; second, reduced government effort to support agriculture; and third, shift of consumer demand to crops not produced domestically.

It has been shown that government policies with regard to the distribution of food aid are the dominant factors in determining the actual effect on domestic production (25). On the other hand, it is now widely admitted that food aid can also have positive effects on domestic agriculture.

To avoid adverse effects of food aid on food production in the recipient country, certain conditions have to be fulfilled:

  i) Non-substitution of food aid for established domestic supplies. This would be the case where food aid substitutes only for a domestic shortfall or where additional supplies are met with additional demand, or are channelled separately into additional consumption.

 ii) Food aid does not reduce the effort deployed by a government to maintain and develop domestic production.

iii) Food aid does not divert consumers from food products which are, or can be, produced domestically.

These conditions are not easy to meet in all cases, and the degree to which they are met is difficult to establish. The non-fulfilment of certain conditions is, on the contrary, easier to prove since, in practice, food aid may be diverted. To the extent that non-respect of the conditions is only marginal, the adverse effects of food aid may be acceptable, although the quantitative impact is difficult to assess.

The first condition concerns the actual flows in the short terms, i.e., the period of supply and distribution, whereas the two other conditions refer to patterns of behaviour extending into the future, which may be influenced not only by food aid but also by numerous other factors. Therefore, a precise causal relationship with food aid supplies can usually not be established. In general, and as with the first condition, only relatively high or concentrated food aid supplies may have a perceptible adverse effect.

Difficulties in fulfilling these conditions completely may be such that it would be vain to concentrate all efforts on them. Countries may actually accept certain adverse effects of food aid on domestic production since they have in any case to be seen against the direct positive effects on consumption (see below).

Building Up Positive Linkages

Positive linkages between food aid and agricultural development are possible when this type of aid can be used to free foreign exchange, mobilise local resources, or serve directly as an input into agriculture.

This potential is not particular to food aid, as distinct from other forms of assistance, but because of the fear that food aid will depress domestic agriculture, it calls for particular emphasis.

The nature of the possible linkages is quite clear, although they may take different forms in different cases. Thus foreign exchange, which would otherwise have been spent to import food, can be used to import capital goods or current inputs to increase agricultural output. Local resources can be mobilised, for example, by distributing food as wages or by using local currency receipts from sales of food aid commodities on the domestic market. Finally, food distributed to labour and farmers in periods of scarcity can secure production for the next season or for later periods in the case of certain investments.

The critical issue is whether the potential linkages become effective and how the transformation can be facilitated.

Food aid as an instrument to free foreign exchange for agricultural development can work in various ways. First, if already established general and sectoral policies are upheld, the additional foreign exchange availability may permit accelerated agricultural development. Second, the tying of food aid supplies to imported components for agricultural production and development could be envisaged, but this might be counterproductive on several counts: it could lead to an uneconomic pattern of investment; it could lead to resentment if not outright rejection by recipient countries; it could be accommodated without any increase in the allocation of foreign currency to agriculture because of the fungibility of financial resources.

Thus, tying of foreign exchange savings from food aid to imports for agricultural development would in most cases appear to be undesirable and ineffective. The general and sectoral policies of the recipient country will therefore have to determine the proper use of such foreign exchange savings. How such policies can be strengthened and assisted from outside will be an important issue in the design and implementation of food sector strategies for specific countries, but it is not related in any special way to the provision of food aid.

Mobilising local resources with food aid poses some of the same problems but may be easier to achieve because it can be applied to a wider scope of activities. These may range from "food-for-work" projects to the use of counterpart funds in agricultural development projects for infrastructure and may include, at the margin, education and health activities. Whether the mobilisation of local resources becomes effective depends on two issues: additionality and practicability. Only if activities funded with food aid resources are additional to what would have been undertaken otherwise can one actually talk of mobilisation of resources. The above argument of fungibility applies.

Quantification of these kinds of links will always have to be made on the basis of some assumption of "what would have happened otherwise". Counterpart funds have been a controversial subject for some time (26). The main arguments against them reflect doubts about the possibility of achieving additionality. Furthermore, where they have been set up, they have rarely been used in a particularly effective way.

Food aid as input into agriculture. The distinction between this category and the preceding one lies in the fact that food aid alone and directly can, in certain cases, be used to increase agricultural output. Grains as seeds, food for nourishment of farmers and animals are the most obvious examples. The distinction is less clear when it comes to food-for-work projects directly related to agriculture, since they will generally require complementary inputs. By definition, these projects are relatively simple but also limited in scope. Here, the issues of additionality may be answered more easily than in other cases.

So far, this section has not distinguished between different types of agriculture or different groups of farmers. Food aid, and in particular project food aid, can be used selectively, and perhaps more effectively than other forms of aid, to reach the poorest sections of the population. This applies particularly where a "poverty stigma" is attached to the kind of aid provided. Thus, if the objective of food aid is not only to promote output but also to improve the distribution of agricultural production, it may have an edge over other types of assistance. Furthermore, focussing on the poorest people, it may stimulate demand for domestically-produced food.

5. FOOD IMPORTS AND CONSUMERS

The impact of food imports on consumers is generally positive in terms of overall availability, but does not solve all problems. It is not sufficient to reason in terms of overall or regional availability. As Sen shows, famines have occurred even when there has been no substantial fall in food availability (27). The main question is whether food imports actually reach those suffering from a deficiency. This raises issues of purchasing power, of effective and timely distribution and of quality of food products; these issues have to be examined at sub-national level for both commercial and concessional supplies.

a) Distribution pattern of food aid

Seen against the needs of hungry people, food aid is considered positively even by many who are rather critical of aid in general. This is most obvious in the case of emergency supplies in connection with natural or man-made calamities. However, the composition of food aid supplies does not fully correspond to the most urgent needs (28).

Food aid supplies had their origin in the United States' surpluses of the 1950s, but since then the element of surplus disposal has considerably weakened everywhere, except perhaps for dairy products from the European Community. However, fluctuations in food aid supply can be explained at least partly in terms of the world market situation. When grain prices were relatively high between 1972 and 1974, food aid supplies fell from 13 million tons to approximately 6 million tons per year (29). In other words, at a time when the financial burden of food imports was particularly high, the relief provided by food aid decreased globally. Two mutually-supportive mechanisms were at work to bring about this result, both contradicting the humanitarian objectives of food aid. First, it appears that some countries preferred to sell their grain on the world market rather than to maintain food aid supplies (30). Second, to the extent that food aid planning and commitments are in value terms, higher food prices mean lower quantities. The Food Aid Convention, however, stipulates commitments in volume rather than value, and in this connection, it is noteworthy that a decline of food aid supplies did not occur for EEC cereal aid between 1971-1972 and 1973-1974, when volume increased by 24 per cent and value by 233 per cent (31).

In 1981-1982 overall cereal food aid supplies of around 10 million tons amounted to approximately 10 per cent of total cereal imports by developing countries. This share was much higher around 1960 and has steadily declined since, making developing countries increasingly reliant on commercial imports. Seen against total imports of agricultural products by all developing countries of $50 billion in 1979 (32), food aid supplies are even less important, with a share of approximately 4 per cent.

Even if the overall importance of food aid in agricultural trade, and thus in meeting food needs, is declining, its role is still considerable, in particular when it goes to the poorest countries and sections of the population. While it is true that the share of food aid supplied to least developed countries (LLDCs) has increased in recent years, most of the food aid goes to countries other than LLDCs and a large share is concentrated in a small number of countries (see Table 14). Thus, food aid to Egypt, which is not among the very poorest countries, is about ten times higher than indicated by its share in LDC population.

Bangladesh seems to have been a privileged food aid recipient in both absolute and relative terms and is, with a GNP per capita of $90 (1979), among the very poorest countries. Yet, considerations of consumer needs do not always dominate in the allocation of food aid. It is by now well documented (33) that food aid supplies to Bangladesh were held back for political reasons in 1974 when the country was faced with a very serious food shortage which led to mass starvation: "The hard lesson of this experience was that food aid supplies, even from friendly foreign countries, cannot be relied upon and that even an inadvertent breaking of rules set by the supplying countries can lead to extreme deprivation" (34). Similar evidence is available with respect to Canadian food aid, showing that domestic interests tend to prevail over LDC requirements (35). In fact, this tends to be a general characteristic of bilateral food aid supplies (36). It is generally found, however,

Table 14

DISTRIBUTION OF FOOD AID FROM DAC MEMBER COUNTRIES(1)

	Population in 1979		Disbursements in $ million and per cent				
	Million	%	1977	1978	1979	1980	1981
All LDCs	2 278.15	100.00	1 686.00	1 630.00	1 895.00	1 970.00	2 306.00
LLDCs	268.20		315.00	385.00	448.00	555.00	685.00
LLDCs (percentage)		11.77	18.70	23.40	23.40	28.20	29.70
Bangladesh	86.93		191.00	183.00	250.00	198.00	206.00
Bangladesh (percentage)		3.81	11.33	11.23	13.19	10.10	8.90
LLDCs without Bangladesh	181.07		124.00	218.00	182.00	357.00	479.00
LLDCS without Bangladesh (percentage)		7.95	7.35	13.37	9.60	18.10	20.80
Other Major Per Capital Recipients							
Egypt	40.85		207.00	224.00	364.00	283.00	409.00
Egypt (percentage)		1.79	12.28	13.74	19.21	14.30	17.70
Indonesia	138.90		128.00	167.00	266.00	173.00	82.00
Indonesia (percentage)		6.10	7.59	10.25	14.04	8.80	3.50
Pakistan	78.54		61.00	73.00	38.00	83.00	143.00
Pakistan (percentage)		3.45	3.62	4.48	2.00	4.20	6.20
3 countries' sub-total	258.29		396.00	464.00	668.00	539.00	633.00
3 countries' sub-total (percentage)		11.34	23.49	28.47	35.25	27.30	27.40

1. DAC countries account for virtually all food aid (apart from a few deliveries by Argentina, India and the USSR; the figures exclude disbursements from multilateral sources other than the EEC.

Source: OECD

that political considerations interfere less with the distribution of food aid from multilateral organisations.

Even if food aid is at times used as a political lever, this does not prevent it from being of great value to consumers who actually receive such food. For consumers as a whole, however, the net positive effect depends on aid supplies being additional to normal supplies and not simply displacing commercial imports. On this point, "most evidence suggests that some displacement occurs" (37).

As explained in an earlier section, food aid supplied on a grant basis and sold in the market will lower consumer prices and at the same time provide counterpart funds with which domestic producers can be subsidised. If the funds thus made available are of sufficient size and stability to increase the productivity of domestic agriculture in the longer run, it will be possible eventually to satisfy domestic demand by domestic supplies and even at lower prices. Thus it is possible in theory, though difficult in practice, to use food aid to bridge the period necessary to increase productivity with benefits accruing to both consumers and domestic producers.

b) Reaching consumers most in need

While political considerations may at times dominate the humanitarian objective of food aid, it is up to the receiving country to decide how far nutritional need should be the decisive criterion for distribution within the country. Nutritional need is generally tantamount to economic need, and the poorest people tend to suffer most from inadequate food intake. Several questions have to be raised at this point. First, if poverty, i.e., lack of effective demand, is the cause of nutritional deficiency, are food aid imports necessary to improve the satisfaction of food needs? Second, is nutritional need indeed the only criterion used for the distribution of food aid within countries? Third, what are the most appropriate ways to distribute food aid from the point of view of nutritional effectiveness?

Where additional domestic food supply exists (but is beyond effective demand) or can be mobilised quickly, food aid does not have to rely on food imports. On the contrary, imports should be avoided and the nutritional needs met with food procured locally. In this case, foreign aid would properly take the form of financial resources for domestic food procurement; it would have no element of surplus disposal by the donor but would simply represent a transfer of resources on humanitarian grounds. It is a relatively new instrument and has been tried as part of German bilateral assistance in Gambia, Niger and Tanzania (38). Locally-procured food aid can have the advantage of being cheaper (this was the case in Gambia and Niger), and it presents no problems with regard to local consumption habits or the mobilisation of otherwise under-utilised local resources. It must be considered as the most desirable form of food aid because it reconciles consumers' and producers' interests, has the potential of making itself unnecessary in the long run by strengthening local agriculture, and avoids the risk of negative side effects such as increased external dependence and the creation of consumption habits which are incompatible with domestic agricultural production.

The questions of who should receive food aid within a country and in which way are interlinked. The first may be answered on ethical grounds, whereas the second raises issues of efficiency. Given the underlying humanitarian objective, the nutritionally most-vulnerable sections of the population should clearly be the privileged recipients of food aid. Nevertheless, particularly in cases of bulk supply of food aid, a first and often large share goes to government employees (39). This has meant continued hardship for the poorest consumers in Bangladesh at times of a short supply of food aid because "a large fixed amount of subsidised food was distributed to government employees and urban populations irrespective of their income levels, while the most vulnerable and poorest rural populations had only residual claims on the grain available at the disposal of the government" (40).

While donor institutions have been known to press for a distribution based on the most urgent needs, it sometimes seems to be considered inopportune to press too hard. As with other resources, the distribution of food aid supplies within a country reflects the interests of those in power and cannot be radically changed without questioning the entire power structure. Furthermore, even if considered unsatisfactory from a donor's point of view with regard to equity, a distribution pattern can still have some positive spillover to the poorest people and is therefore preferable on humanitarian grounds to a situation where no food aid at all reaches the poorest. Indirect (price) effects of food aid to the "not-so-needy" may add to the spillover and further justify maintaining food aid supplies despite a situation of unsatisfactory distribution.

An ideal distribution pattern may be out of reach, but there are ways and means of targeting food aid which help to reach a larger share of the poorest people than if no such efforts are made. One way is the so-called "self-targeting" which obtains when an inferior commodity (usually consumed only by the poor) is selected for food aid. Certain grains or root crops may come under this category but it will be difficult to make this kind of distinction in certain situations (41). Another way of targeting food aid supplies to poorer groups consists of projects in which food is distributed on the principle of "food for wages" of "food for nutrition" (42). Targeting may take place by means of project location, by type and timing of work, or by specific designation of beneficiaries of supplementary feeding (e.g. pregnant and lactating women or preschool children).

Supplementary feeding projects have been shown to be "truly additional" in some countries. On the other hand, where food is supplied for wages, it may simply replace income from other sources and consequently additionality is less frequently assured (43). Supplementary feeding programmes directed towards women and small children have been reported as having a significant nutritional impact (44).

Food distribution targeted to the poorest sections of the population is nutritionally cost-effective, as measured in terms of the cost per additional unit of food consumed by the under-nourished group (45). However, the concrete delineation of the target group, a high degree of coverage and the prevention of leakages of subsidised food beyond the intended beneficiaries can be difficult and costly tasks. Detailed knowledge about the situation of the poor, and considerable administrative and financial capacities, are necessary to cope with them. In any case, there should be no illusions about solving all the problems with closely targeted administrative measures. "While these may be excellent in conception, they may face such enormous obstacles through bureaucratic confusion and corruption that it is preferable to use the price mechanism even if it spreads benefits to others than those in the most extreme need; the bureaucracy may in fact channel resources in the wrong direction to a far greater extent" (46).

Without necessarily subscribing to so wholesale a condemnation of administrative targeting of food aid, it may be worth examining briefly how, and to what extent, market forces can be expected to allocate food to the poor (47). Increased overall supply through food aid will tend to depress food prices. Since poor people spend a high share of their income on food, they will benefit relatively more in proportion to their income. High-income consumers spend relatively less on food, but in absolute terms their expenditure is much higher. Thus, in principle, "the market efficiently allocates the food to the poor [but] it allocates the financial benefits substantially to the rich" (48). The poor may also benefit from indirect employment effects caused by a changed spending pattern on the part of the rich. In any event, if food aid is distributed via the open market because of the simplicity of the procedure, care has to be taken (monitoring and possibly protective measures) to limit the attendant adverse effects.

In conclusion, it seems worth underlining that though the method of distribution of food aid largely determines its effects, there need not be exclusive reliance on one method alone. Release on the market (with certain precautions but for a broader public) can be accompanied by supplementary feeding and food-for-work projects for narrowly defined vulnerable groups (49). This is particularly true in countries with high food deficits where multiple objectives are pursued with food aid.

Finally, a consequence of food aid imports which is often asserted but rarely documented (50) is a change in the consumption habits of consumers and subsequently increased dependence on imports for commodities that cannot be produced domestically. This applies particularly to milk products and wheat, which are traditionally not produced in tropical areas and can at best be introduced only at high cost. However, it appears that changes in consumer taste "can be ascribed to a host of social and economic factors which may or may not include food aid" (51). This makes a quantification of the causal relationship virtually impossible, but the danger is nevertheless real (52).

c) The role of commercial food imports for consumers

In this section we raise three major questions relating to the manner and extent to which consumers are affected by food imports: what are the conditions under which food imports take place (ranging from free trade to restricted imports subject to duties or benefitting from government subsidies); what would be an effective system of distribution; and what type of food products are imported? Consumers are not a homogeneous group and may be affected differently according to their income, geographic location and consumption habits. Unfortunately, the material available hardly allows us to do justice to such differentiation other than in general terms.

Where relatively low food prices fit into the government strategy (53), consumers stand to benefit most from increased food imports because their prices tend to be lower than for domestic supplies (54). Consumers who are not buying imported products may benefit from the imports in an indirect way, via a reduced price level and increased general availability.

A special low food price policy has been followed by Egypt, where cereal imports have increased spectacularly and domestic production has advanced at the same time (see Table 15). This was achieved with subsidised commercial imports (in addition to food aid) which allowed an increase in per capita availability of cereals from about 300 kg. in the early 1960s to 336 kg. in 1979, despite a 50 per cent increase in the population over the same period (55). The financial burden of this kind of import policy is, of course, very heavy and has to be seen against the strong pressure from consumers who threaten political turmoil every time any attempt is made to reduce subsidies. While the Egyptian case is rather extreme with regard to the level of both cereal imports and subsidies, other countries have had similar experiences. Algeria is a case in point - with only temporary subsidisation of imports, however (56).

In the event of domestic production shortfall and insufficient domestic stocks, imports may also be essential for consumers who normally rely on domestic supply. Since subsistence consumption tends to be maintained, fluctuations in marketable surpluses are higher than those of domestic output.

Where a developing country can afford a rising food import bill, e.g. Libya, increasing income is naturally reflected in both increased consumption of traditional products and a diversification in the consumption pattern. However, where the level of food intake is already relatively high, the imports may substitute to some extent for traditional food products. This seems to have happened in the Ivory Coast, where wheat, rice and maize (though not all imported) partly substituted for the traditional root crops.

Table 15

DOMESTIC PRODUCTION AND IMPORTS OF CEREALS IN EGYPT
(in 1 000 tonnes)

	1961/ 1964	1965/ 1967	1970/ 1974	1975	1976	1977	1978	1979	1980	1981
Cereal production (1)	6 112	6 789	7 750	8 179	8 193	7 460	8 269	8 068	8 120	7 795
Cereal imports (2)	1 913	2 274	2 080	3 382	3 378	4 935	5 961	5 400	6 376	7 287
(2) in % of (1)	31	33	27	41	41	66	72	67	79	93

Source: FAO Production and Trade Yearbooks, various editions.

A more ambiguous issue is that of who actually benefits from additional food imports. This largely depends on the distribution system, on income and on consumption habits, all of which tend to bring about privileged access of urban consumers to imported food. Distribution channels cover urban areas better than rural areas, income tends to be higher in urban areas, and urban consumers have a stronger preference for imported foods, be it for their taste and prestige or for convenience of preparation.

While this distortion may result from poor infrastructure and high internal transport cost, it may also be due to weaknesses in the implementation of distribution systems and even general government policies. In Egypt, for example, the administered prices are less well enforced in the rural areas than in the cities, with the consequence that "frequently, merchants and rural people, when in urban cities on business, buy subsidised commodities either for their own consumption or for profitable resale in rural markets" (57). Wheat and flour imports are a State monopoly under the authority of the Egyptian Organisation of Milling, which supplies public mills and bakeries mainly located in urban areas; the latter are thus the main beneficiaries of both food imports and subsidies (58). In Algeria, too, cereal imports come under a State monopoly and are channelled mainly to urban areas where they meet consumers' needs at low cost in two ways. First, they provide cereals for direct consumption (bread, flour, semolina) by the poorer sections of the population, and second, indirectly, they satisfy the demand of better-off consumers for meat, which is produced locally by feeding imported grains to animals (59). However, as can be seen from Table 16, wheat imports have grown in such a way that an increasing share can be made available to rural consumers.

Another example of food imports under State monopoly and public food grain distribution is provided by Sri Lanka. It has been shown (60) that in this country, contrary to the experience of Egypt, Algeria and other developing countries, consumers of different income groups and regions benefitted in a remarkably even way from the general food distribution. The nutritional impact was even greater for poorer consumers due to their higher marginal propensity to spend on calories. While the system was sustainable under the conditions of low import prices for food in the 1950s and 1960s, it became an increasing burden due to the higher world market prices of the 1970s which in 1978 led to the limitation of benefits to the poorer half of the population.

Finally, the question of the role of food imports for consumers has to be addressed also in terms of the nature of the food products which are being imported. Some authors argue that the food industry attempts to change food habits so as to be able to increase its sales (61). While this is an aspect of conventional marketing strategies, there is also a certain inertia in consumption patterns, reflecting taste, income and tradition. Thus, consumption patterns of staples seem to change only very slowly, but this does not exclude dramatic changes at the margin with regard to non-essential foods or very specific cases. Nutritionally undesirable effects may be the consequence in some cases; in others, however, increased consumption, for example, of meat (imported directly or indirectly) and other imported products represents a clear improvement of the diet (62). On the other hand, consumers' persistent preference for traditional products (e.g. certain varieties of rice in the case of Korea) is reflected in the acceptance of higher prices for these products and in the difficulties encountered in selling imported rice once the shortage of domestic supplies has been overcome.

Clearly, where imports consist of relatively expensive products (e.g. meat) or are intended for animal feeding rather than human consumption, they will mainly benefit the better-off consumers. The end-use of imported food is not always easy to determine on the basis of trade statistics, since most grains can be used for several purposes. Thus it may happen that, in spite of increasing food imports, the nutritional situation of certain consumers

Table 16

IMPORTS AND URBAN CONSUMPTION OF WHEAT IN ALGERIA
(in 1000 tonnes)

	Urban Consumption	Imports
1970	951.96	244.74
1971	952.12	539.32
1972	952.12	920.91
1973	952.12	793.30
1974	983.54	1 616.71
1975	1 266.15	1 855.39

Source: H. Delorme, "L'Algérie: importations de céréales, blocage de la production et développement de l'Etat", in Maghred Machrek, No. 91, 1981, p. 16.

deteriorates. It has been argued that the Mexican experience during the 1970s provides an example of this.

With growing populations, even unchanged consumption patterns can lead to increased imports and thus growing food dependence. To the extent that consumption patterns include products which are produced locally, this problem is exacerbated. Growing food dependence is considered a serious problem by many developing countries whose perception of and reactions to the problem will be examined in the following chapter.

6. MASTERING FOOD IMPORTS

While food imports are desirable in most cases from a consumer's point of view, many developing countries have declared increased food self-sufficiency as one of their priority objectives. This is true not only for the poorest countries such as those of the Sahel (63), but also for oil-exporting countries like Venezuela, Mexico, Indonesia and Nigeria. The aim is mainly to decrease import dependence for staple crops. Indonesia has widened its objective of self-sufficiency in rice to more general food self-sufficiency (including maize, cassava, soya, sweet potatoes). As long as total self-sufficiency is not achieved, continued access to imported grain supplies on terms that developing countries can afford is of the greatest importance.

Poorer countries have to limit food imports for lack of foreign exchange but there are also other reasons, stated more or less explicitly. Thus, in the case of Venezuela, it is explicitly recognised that industrialisation cannot provide employment for the rapidly-growing urban population and, therefore, that increasing domestic food production must be relied upon to slow down rural-urban migration, making fuller use of domestic resources and reducing food imports at the same time (64).

The Risks of Food Dependence

More generally, it has been argued that "it is one of the lessons learned again in the 1970s that certain degrees of self-sufficiency are a necessary insurance against extreme risks" (65). Risks related to the geographic concentration of the world's exportable surpluses have been the focus of increasing attention recently (66). These risks are environmental as well as political. First, it has been argued that "levels of future production are more at risk from climatic factors than recent experience would suggest" (67). Second, in a report investigating the 1970 US maize blight, the US National Academy of Sciences recognised that "most major crops are impressively uniform and impressively vulnerable" (68). Third, the risk of contamination from a major accident or sabotage of a nuclear reactor cannot be excluded since it could lead to withdrawal or restrictions on the use of crops grown in the contaminated area (69).

As to political risk, fear of the use of "food power" has often been mentioned recently and seems to underlie some of the reasoning for increased food self-sufficiency. Without wishing to overstate its practical relevance in the context of food import policies, the concept of food power is elaborated upon here to clarify some of the issues which tend to be submerged in emotional discussions and ad hoc arguments.

The structural conditions necessary for one country to exercise food power over another are presented by Wallensteen (70) and can be summarised as follows:

1. Scarcity: the commodity or commodity group in question must have at least short-term limitations (usually physical) to increased supply. When coupled with a high and rising absolute demand, competition for supply can lead to purchasers being obliged to pay high prices and even to make political concessions. Although this is the primary condition for the exercise of food power, it is a necessary but not a sufficient condition.

2. Supply concentration: there must be a limited number of producers or sellers; again this is a necessary but not a sufficient condition. As in the case of OPEC, this condition is most clearly associated with a cartel which controls a commodity at its source.

3. Demand dispersion: assuming conditions 1 and 2, it is also necessary that there be no effective countervailing concentration of demand.

4. Action independence: the supplier must not be vulnerable to retaliation either directly, in respect of the commodity in question, or indirectly via trade in other commodities.

If these conditions are met, then the supplier possesses a structural possibility to utilise the economic asset as a political instrument. Stress should be placed on the word "possibility". Political alliances, trade ties or other considerations may override the actual use of the potential.

Wallensteen concludes that, given the fulfilment of these conditions, the United States possesses not food power but grain power. It should be added, however, that these conditions are not necessarily sufficient effectively to exercise power (i.e. impose one's will) in all cases. Wallensteen admits that food power alone, whether used as an incentive or as a disincentive, has not been effective in the longer run in cases where it has met with firm and broadly-based opposition, because there are ways and means of circumventing it (71).

In a more limited analysis of Wallensteen's four conditions of food power for the United States and Canada, and adding the condition of co-operation among major exporters, Cohn (72) reaches a similar conclusion.

Nevertheless, serious damage can be done in the short run (73). Combined with other political forces, the objective pursued with food power may be achieved. But there are also examples to show that this has not always been possible (74).

Even if food exporters could derive benefits from keeping developing countries heavily dependent on food imports, this could turn out to be a very shortsighted strategy, because in the longer run, exporting countries could probably not satisfy needs under the conditions thus created (75). Therefore, well-perceived mutual interests of both food exporting and importing countries would suggest that, for the longer run and as a general rule (which needs differentiation from country to country, of course), a strategy of developing local food-producing capacity should be followed. This is not an argument for autarchy; the aim is to avoid aggravating imbalances which would most likely lead to untenable future import dependence.

Analysing international food trade and production from a free trade perspective, and suspicious of the objective of self-sufficiency, Josling (76) comes to a similar conclusion. He notes that by taxing their agriculture, developing countries keep production lower than would otherwise be the case. He further suggests that productivity of increased investment in agriculture may be greater in developing countries than in developed countries. Thus, "the resource cost of producing food could be reduced for the world as a whole by encouraging production in developing rather than in developed regions" (77). In countries where this applies, international assistance for investment in food production could be justified in terms of an economically more rational location of world food production.

Scope and Avenues for Reduced Food Dependence

Acknowledging the economic and political implications of food imports, each country has to consider the options open to it: strengthening its food import capacity (by increased exports, possibly combined with a greater diversification of sources of imports, as well as improved procurement systems and import infrastructure, notably port, storage and transport (facilities), or expanding domestic food production. It should be noted that these options are not necessarily exclusive but may be combined in a more complex set of policies, for example, by differentiating according to products or product groups. For some products, the emphasis may be on unrestricted imports subject to duties, the fiscal revenue therefrom being applied to promote domestic production of other crops which may be subject to import restrictions. The choices are difficult. Because different trade and production policies are likely to affect various groups of the population in different ways, the strategy adopted will have to reflect both economic factors (e.g. domestic resource cost and world market conditions) and internal socio-political constellations such as:

1. Domestic food supply and demand conditions;

2. Food import conditions and prospects;

3. Import capacity (actual and potential foreign exchange earnings);

4. Development strategy (relative weight, nature and distribution of investment and consumption);

5. Internal political situations (e.g. need to satisfy particular constituencies);

6. Domestic resource use and production potential;

7. Scope for external resources transfer (commercial and concessional).

These factors are themselves amenable to further differentiation and may vary in importance over time. They explain why even countries in similar ecological and economic situations, such as the countries of the Sahel region (see Section 2 in this chapter), show quite different import patterns.

Theoretically, a country's import policy could be designed on the basis of a systematic and explicit examination of all the above factors. More typical, however, are policy changes in reaction to changes in the configuration of these factors. Thus, the Ivory Coast launched its policy for rice self-sufficiency in 1974 after the food crisis of 1972-73 when rice prices skyrocketed on the world market.

A few countries have launched campaigns for increased self-reliance in food. Ghana's "Operation Feed Yourself" (OFY)", initiated in 1972, is an early example (78). However, its concentration on large-scale operations such as commercial and State farms and the Food Corporation has turned out to be rather inefficient. While food imports have been reduced, this was achieved at a very high cost, making locally-produced rice prohibitively expensive for many consumers. In fact, locally-produced foodstuffs became more expensive than most imported food items.

From the outset, small farmers were neglected in the OFY Programme. Girdner et al. note that there was a structural bias against small farmers in two ways. First, as in many countries, the Agricultural Development Bank would grant loans only upon proof of legal title to the land. But much of the land in Ghana is communally owned and specific parcels are farmed by individual family units under grant from the village chief. Second, the onerous bureaucracy in Accra is both physically and socially distant from peasant farmers.

Another example of a nationwide campaign to reduce food imports is provided by Nigeria's "Operation Feed the Nation (OFN)" which was launched in 1976. The major objective of the OFN is food self-sufficiency by 1985. This overall plan, plus the supporting National Accelerated Food Production

Project (NAPP), calls for a "green revolution" transformation of Nigerian food production. The two constitute a nationwide integrated programme of research, extension and provision of modern technical inputs (fertilizers, pesticides, improved seeds, etc.) to the masses of Nigerian small-scale producers. The initial phase of the plan concentrates on rice, maize and sorghum, millet, wheat and cassava, rice and maize being the two most important (79). The plan also proposes elements of self-help (especially in grain storage), popular participation in decision-making, a student corps to assist in extension work and a heavy emphasis on local -- even urban -- self-sufficiency ("grow your own") in small-scale food production.

Agricultural input and output prices are being revised by the Federal Price Control Board to reflect more fully real costs; moreover, a detailed programme of input price subsidies is being pursued under the NAPP. In addition, since 1978, banks have been required to grant 6 per cent of new loans to the agricultural sector; any shortfalls must be deposited at the Central Bank at no interest.

In order to protect domestic production, the Government is also tenaciously pursuing restrictions on certain food imports. Rice is a good example of the range of efforts being undertaken. In 1978, the Government imposed a ban on rice imports of less than 50 kilograms (to achieve scale economies in operations and cut out excessive import consumption), then all import licenses were centralised within the Central Bank. Finally, in 1979, rice imports were banned in toto.

Preliminary results of the OFN programme indicated a mixed picture. Rice and maize, two of the favoured staples under the OFN, have fared well. Domestic rice production in 1979 was up almost 50 per cent over 1976, a threefold increase over the 1961-65 period. Maize output was about one-quarter greater in 1979 than in 1976. The more traditional crops -- millet and sorghum -- remained stagnant if not declining in terms of year-to-year production figures, and domestic wheat production was insignificant compared to newly-emerging demand. Abalu and D'Silva noted in the third year of the OFN programme that it was suffering from the Government's inability to make available the needed inputs in the right quantities and at the right place and time" (80). A similarly critical assessment was made by Wallace who noted that Nigerian agricultural policy primarily aims at the largest farmers and ignores the mass of the rural population. In his opinion, the large-scale schemes relying on sophisticated technology and bureaucratic management are doomed to failure (81).

Zaire reacted to the acceleration of food imports during the 1970s (especially the doubling of imports of maize, its second most important staple) with an Agricultural Recovery Plan (82) which discusses past policy shortcomings and proposes new priorities. However, its neglect of the large traditional food sector, of linkages in the food system and poor implementation prospects seem to make its success unlikely.

A large number of other developing countries are also making efforts to improve domestic food supply, with or without attempting to substitute domestic production for food imports. Such policies are based on the assumption that the necessary physical inputs, infrastructure, knowledge and incentives are available when and where required. Effective demand, which is a necessary condition of success, is obviously easier to assess in the case of import substitution, subject to the condition that domestic produce is identical or comparable in quality to the previously imported products. If this is not the case, the new domestic production may need very high protection. But instead of discouraging or banning imports completely, it may be advisable, in theory, to split the demand and make high-income consumers pay for their preference for an imported product (via duties) while other consumers rely on domestic production which might be promoted with the funds derived from import duties. On a practical level, this may not be feasible, however.

By applying a selective policy of import substitution and production promotion, paying due attention to both the comparative advantage of the country and the implications for different categories of producers and consumers, it may be feasible to reconcile conflicting interests at reasonable cost.

Because of the nutritional and political importance of staple crops, these often receive special protection. This may be in contradiction with the evolution of the country's comparative advantage and thus imply ever-increasing cost to consumers and taxpayers. Anderson sees this happening in Korea and Taiwan and therefore argues that "their most efficient adjustment would be towards producing more naturally-protected products such as fruit and vegetables and perhaps chicken, eggs and pork, rather than beef, dairy products and feedgrains" (83).

Recognising that certain imported foodstuffs (e.g. wheat, beef) cannot (or only at very high cost) be produced in certain developing countries, it is sometimes recommended to replace them by traditional products after a promotion effort (e.g. research for increased productivity and consumer acceptability). While this may be nutritionally desirable and economically sound in countries with a very limited production and export potential, it implies a certain degree of austerity on the part of at least some groups of consumers. However, this may be the price to be paid to correct imbalances and to move towards development with more equity.

Domestic production shortfalls and related import needs are not necessarily the consequence of the weather or of other factors which cannot be controlled. They can also result from policy mistakes. Tandon (84) argues, for example, that the 1980 maize crisis in Kenya was a consequence of errors in the production, storage and export policies pursued in the preceding years. Thus, due to government purchase and storage of large quantities of maize from the bumper crop of 1976-77, only small quantities could be brought in the following year. As a consequence, farmers faced marketing problems in 1977-78 and reduced their maize acreage in 1978-79. A smaller harvest was therefore to be expected, but the Government continued exporting from its stocks in 1979 and had great difficulties in meeting domestic demand with imports in 1980. This underlines the critical importance of the timing of policy measures.

In conclusion, mastering food imports will require adjustments in the domestic food system and in the policies concerning it. But there are physical, economic, and sometimes political, limits to such adjustments which are different in each country and have to be identified as clearly as possible to improve policy-making. However, in a dynamic context, these limits can be expected to change. Therefore, the situation has to be monitored, and adjustment has to be conceived not as a once-for-all operation but as a process which can change in nature over time. To the extent that food imports are necessary and maintained, they may also be subject to adjustment in terms of composition and origin. Thus, a recent UNIDO study (85) suggests that import substitution in the food processing industry should be promoted. It is argued, for example, that grain processing would allow savings from importing bulk grain instead of flour. The experience of Saudi Arabia is cited as a successful example. Diversification in the sources of food imports may reduce some risks dealt with earlier on; the added costs and complications of such diversification have to be weighed against the reduced vulnerability and -- in some cases -- the potential long-term benefits from strengthened regional co-operation (86).

NOTES AND REFERENCES

1. Cereal grains account for over 85 per cent of poor countries' food imports in terms of value. See. D.G. Sisler and D. Blanford, Rubber or Rice? -- The Dilemma of Many Developing Nations, World Food Issues Series, Centre for the Analysis of World Food Issues, Cornell University, Ithaca, 1979.

2. FAO, AT 2000 (1981), p. 3; this study contains also estimates of import requirements for 1990 and the year 2000.

3. The outlook is more positive for other food crops.

4. K. Lampe et al., "Agricultural Production: Research and Development Strategies for the 1960s, Conclusions and Recommendations of the Bonn Conference, 8th-12th October 1979", Rockefeller Foundation, 1980, p. 1. For possible ways of saving energy in agriculture, food processing, distribution and preparation, see M.B. Green, Eating Oil, Energy Use in Food Production, Westview Press, Boulder, Colorado, 1979. As for investment needs, see, for example, P. Oram, "The Investment Tripod: Infrastructure, Technology and Training", in IFPRI Report, Vol. 2, No. 1, pp. 1-4. For a more critical view of input-intensive agriculture, denouncing its dependence on imports and environmental side effects, see M. Kiley-Worthington, "Problems of Modern Agriculture", in Food Policy, Vol. 5, No. 3, 1980.

5. K.L. Bachmann, L.A. Paulino, "Rapid Food Production Growth in Selected Developing Countries: A Comparative Analysis of Underlying Trends, 1961-1976", IFPRI Research Report, No. 11, October 1979, p. 59.

6. See UNIDO, "The Importance of Pesticides in Developing Contries", Industrial Production and Formulation of Pesticides in Developing Countries, Vol. I, General Principles and Formulation of Pesticides, 1972.

7. Tractors are the only item of farm machinery on which international trade data (both quantity and value) are provided in the FAO Trade Yearbook.

8. For further discussion, see, for example, H. Singer, "Technologies for Basic Needs", ILO, Geneva, 1977.

9. See N. Jéquier, Appropriate Technology: Problems and Promises, OECD Development Centre, Paris, 1976.

10. World Bank, World Development Report, 1981, Washington, D.C., Annex Table 10.

11. Ibid.

12. The argument runs roughly as follows: if the domestic resource cost per net unit of foreign exchange (a measure for the comparative advantage of a given commodity) is considerably higher for food crops (which can be imported) than for other crops (for which export demand exists), it is profitable for a country to keep up food imports and pay for them with the receipts from export crops which are higher than the import costs. Examples of domestic resource costs per net unit of foreign exchange for export crops and for food crops in selected African countries are given in the World Bank report, Accelerated Development in Sub-Saharan Africa, op. cit.

13. For a similarly inconclusive answer, suggesting the need for further research, see H. Wagstaff, "Food Imports of Developing Countries", in Food Policy, Vol. 7, No. 1, February 1982.

14. Finding of this nature are reported, inter alia, for Korea: see Dong-Hi Kim and Yong-Jae Joo, The Food Situation and Policies in the Republic of Korea, OECD Development Centre, Paris, 1982, pp. 31-32.

15. See, for example, the World Bank, Accelerated Development in Sub-Saharan Africa, op. cit.

16. See Dong-Hi Kim and Yong-Jae Joo, op. cit.

17. For estimates of the effect of price distortions on unemployment and migration, see M.D. Bale and E. Lutz, "Price distortions in Agriculture and Their Effects: An International Comparison", World Bank Staff Working Paper No. 359, Washington, D.C., October 1979.

18. See H. Ait-Amara, "Effets des importations alimentaires sur la structure de la production agricole", paper presented at a meeting of the "Evolution of Food Consumption in Algeria", at the Centre de Recherche en Economie Appliquée, Algiers, June 1981.

19. G.T. Harris, Replacing Imported Food Supplies to Port Moresby, Papua New Guinea, Occasional Paper No. 17, Development Studies Centre, Australian National University, Canberra, 1980.

20. S. Sawadogo, L'Agriculture en Côte d'Ivoire, Presses Universitaires de France, Paris, 1977, p. 167.

21. Ibid. However, Harris reports that a profit margin control for imported foodstuffs was introduced in Papua New Guinea in 1974. See G.T. Harris, op. cit., p. 7.

22. See C. Stevens, Food Aid and the Developing World. Four African Case Studies, Overseas Development Institute, London, 1979, p. 188.

23. For recent country studies and general discussions as well as comprehensive bibliographies, see K.H. Beissner et al., Ernährungssicherungsprogramme einschliesslich Nahrungsmittelhilfe und ihre entwicklungspolitischen Auswirkungen in Empfängerländern, Welforum Verlag, Cologne, 1981; C. Stevens, op. cit.; and H. Schneider, Food Aid for Development, OECD Development Centre, Paris, 1979.

24. See K.H. Beissner et al., op. cit., pp. 166-170.

25. Ibid., p. 171, who came to this conclusion in their review of the literature and found it confirmed in studies which they conducted in the Gambia, Niger and Tanzania.

26. See also H. Schneider, op. cit., pp. 14-15.

27. Amartya Sen, Poverty and Famine, An Essay on Entitlement and Deprivation, Clarendon Press, Oxford, 1981, pp. 162-163.

28. See D. Williams and R. Young, La securité alimentaire -- moisson des années 1980, Essai Nord-Sud No. 3, Institut Nord-Sud, Ottawa, 1981, pp. 60-65.

29. FAO, "Agriculture: Towards 2000", C79/24, July 1979.

30. The decline in value of U.S. food aid under PL 480 in 1973 and 1974 supports this hypothesis; see USDA, Food for Peace, 1978 Annual Report, Washington, D.C., 1979, Table 6.

31. See C. Stevens, op. cit., pp. 33-34.

32. FAO, Trade Yearbook 1979, Table 6.

33. See J. Parkinson, "Food Aid", in J. Faaland (ed.), Aid and Influence, the Case of Bangladesh, MacMillan, London, 1981.

34. Ibid., p. 100.

35. T.H. Cohn, "Canadian Food Aid: Domestic and Foreign Policy Implications", Monograph Series in World Affairs, Graduate school of International Studies, Denver, 1979.

36. J.R. Tarrant, "The Geography of food Aid", in Transactions, Institute of British Geographers, Vol. 5, No. 2, 1980, pp. 125-140.

37. B.J. Deaton, "Public Law 480: The Critical Choices", in American Journal of Agricultural Economics, Vol. 62, No. 5, December 1980, Proceedings Issue, p. 990.

38. K.H. Beissner et al., op. cit

39. Ibid., p. 172 refer to examples from African countries and Bangladesh; for the latter country, the argument is supported with a description of

the functioning of the rationing system by J. Parkinson, op. cit., pp. 83-85.

40.   J. Parkinson, idem; similarly, with more detail on the distribution system, Q.K. Ahmad and M. Hogue, "Food Aid in Bangladesh - Who is it For?", Bangladesh Institute of Development Studies, Dacca, 1980, mimeo.

41.   This possibility applies to food subsidisation in general, whether under food aid arrangements or in a purely national scheme. In the case of Korea it has been recommended to select barley for subsidisation instead of rice. See Dong-Hi Kim and Yong-Jae Joo, op. cit.

42.   See C. Stevens, op. cit., who has coined these terms in preference to the more common "food for work" and feeding projects, and who has reviewed the experience of Botswana, Lesotho, Upper Volta and Tunisia.

43.   Ibid., p. 198.

44.   See S. Lane, "The Contribution of Food Aid to Nutrition", in American Journal of Agricultural Economics, Vol. 62, No. 5, December 1980, Proceedings Issue, pp. 984-987.

45.   See S. Reutlinger and M. Selowsky, "Malnutrition and Poverty: Magnitude and Policy Options", World Bank Occasional Paper No. 23, 1976; and M. Selowsky, "Target Group-Oriented Food Programmes: Cost-Effectiveness Comparisons", in American Journal of Agricultural Economics, Vol. 61, No. 5, December 1979, Proceedings Issue, pp. 988-994.

46.   D. Lehmann, reporting on the Workshop on Impact of Food Price Policies on Nutrition: "Political Framework for Nutrition Policies", in Food and Nutrition Bulletin, Vol. 1, No. 1, United Nations University, October 1978.

47.   See also J.W. Mellor, "Food Aid and Nutrition", in American Journal of Agricultural Economics, Vol. 62, No. 5, December 1980, Proceedings Issue, pp. 979-983.

48.   Ibid., p. 981, who bases this conclusion on data from India.

49.   See H. Schneider, op. cit., pp. 67-68, where this point is derived from the experience in several Asian countries.

50.   See, for example, J. Berthelot and F. de Ravignan, Les sillons de la faim, textes rassemblés par le Groupe de la Déclaration de Rome, L'Harmattan, Paris, 1980, p. 110, and S. Lane, op. cit., p. 984.

51.   C. Stevens, op. cit., p. 148.

52.   The general point has also been made in a recent review of Swiss food aid which concludes that locally-unknown food products should not be used and that increased attention should be paid to local food habits and to local procurement wherever possible. See J. Schertenleib, "Schweizer Nahrungsmittelhilfe - Begründung, Wirkungen, Postulate", Entwicklungspolitische Diskussionsbeiträge No. 21, Institut für Sozialethik des SEK Entwicklungsstudien, Adliswil, 1981.

53. See, for example, G.T. Harris, op. cit., p. 7, with regard to Papua New Guinea.

54. This may be the result of a highly-productive agriculture in other countries or of distortions such as surplus disposal by the exporting economy or an over-valued currency in the importing country.

55. For more detail on the Egyptian import and distribution policy see L. Tubiana, "L'Egypte: agriculture, alimentation et géopolitiques des échanges", in Maghreb Machrek, No. 91, 1981, pp. 22-42, and A.A. Goueli, "Food Security Programme in Egypt", in A. Valdès (ed.), Food Security for Developing Countries, Westview Press, Boulder, Colorado, 1981, pp. 143-157.

56. See H. Delorme, "L'Algérie: importations de céréales, blocage de la production et développement de l'Etat", in Maghreb Machrek, No. 91, 1981, pp. 7-23.

57. A.A. Goueli, op. cit., p. 151

58. See L. Tubiana, op. cit., pp. 35-36.

59. See H. Delorme op. cit., p. 11.

60. See J.D. Gavan and I.S. Chandrasekera, "The Impact of Public Foodgrain Distribution on Food Consumption and Welfare in Sri Lanka", IFPRI Research Report No. 13, Washington, D.C., December 1978.

61. See S. George, Les stratèges de la faim, Editions Grounauer, Geneva, 1981, pp. 175-184.

62. This is most noticeable in countries where per capita income has risen strongly. For Korea, see Dong-Hi Kim and Yong Jae-Joo, op. cit., p. 20.

63. The CILSS/Club du Sahel strategy aims at self-sufficiency for the essential food needs by the end of the century; Senegal has more precise and medium-term objectives in its 1981-1985 Plan, e.g. for import substitution with regard to sugar, tomato concentrate, vegetables and grains. For the latter, a reduction of rice consumption of 40 per cent is targeted for 1985, presumably to be substituted by locally-produced maize.

64. See E. Sposito and M. Medina, "La réduction de la dépendance agro-alimentaire, cas du Vénézuéla", in Cahiers du CENECA, Agriculture et Alimentation, International Colloquium, Paris, March 1981.

65. A. Weber, "The Various Concepts of Self-Sufficiency and International Trade", in Quarterly Journal of International Agriculture, Vol. 20, No. 3, 1981, pp. 247-248.

66. See, for example, H. Wagstaff, op. cit., pp. 57-68.

67. Ibid., p. 66.

68. U.S. National Academy of Sciences, <u>Genetic Vulnerability of Major Crops</u>, Washington, D.C., 1972, p. 1, cited in H. Wagstaff, op. cit., p. 66.

69. See H. Wagstaff, <u>op. cit</u>., p. 67.

70. P. Wallensteen, "Scarce Goods as Political Weapons: The Case of Food", in V. Harle (ed.), <u>The Political Economy of Food</u>, Saxon House, Farnborough, 1978.

71. See P. Wallensteen, <u>op. cit</u>., pp. 88-93.

72. See T.H. Cohn, <u>op. cit</u>., p. 99.

73. Witness the experience of Bangladesh related earlier in this report

74. See H. Tuomi, "Food Imports and Neo-Colonialism", in V. Harle (ed.), <u>op. cit</u>., pp. 1-22, who refers to the example of U.S. food aid for Indochina.

75. On this point see L. Soth, "The Grain Export Boom: Should it be Tamed?", in <u>Foreign Affairs</u>, Spring 1981, pp. 895-912.

76. T. Josling, "International Trade and World Food Production", in D.G. Johnson (ed.), <u>The Politics of Food</u>, The Chicago Council on Foreign Relations, Chicago, 1980, pp. 36-59.

77. <u>Ibid</u>., p. 44.

78. For a detailed assessment on which we draw here, see J. Girdner et al., in <u>Food Policy</u>, Vol. 5, No. 1, 1980, pp. 14-25.

79. Details of various projections and alternative objectives are given in: The Federal Ministry of Agriculture, <u>Agricultural Development in Nigeria</u>: 1973-1985, Lagos, 1974.

80. G.O.I. Abalu and B. D'Silva, "Nigeria's Food Situation - Problems and Prospects", in <u>Food Policy</u>, Vol. 5, No. 1, February 1980, pp. 49-60.

81. T. Wallace, "The Challenge of Food: Nigeria's Approach to Agriculture 1975-1980", in <u>Canadian Journal of African Studies</u>, Vol. 15, No. 2, 1981, pp. 239-258.

82. Département du Plan, Programme de Relance Agricole, 1978-1980, Kinshasa, 1978.

83. K. Anderson, "Changing Comparative Advantage in Agriculture: Theory and Pacific Basin Experience", in <u>Journal of Rural Development</u>, Vol. III, No. 2, December 1980, pp. 213-234.

84. See Y. Tandon, "New Food Strategies and Social Transformation in East Africa", in <u>Africa Development</u>, CODESRIA, Vol. VI, No. 2, 1981, pp. 86-106.

85. UNIDO, "First Global Study on the Food Processing Industry", ID/WG-345/3, August 1981.

86. The latter is expected to result, for example, from the Regional Food Plan of the Caribbean. See the Caribbean Community Secretariat, CARICOM Feeds Itself, Georgetown, 1977.

Chapter IV

DOMESTIC STRUCTURAL CHANGE AND POLICY OPTIONS

INTRODUCTION

The context of change on which this study places emphasis is not only determined by the export and import activities dealt with earlier on, but also by the domestic production potential, economic interests and power relationships within the country. Brief reference to these domestic factors has been made at various points in the preceding chapters. For the sake of a balanced presentation, issues and mechanisms of domestic structural change are reviewed here to underline their major role in many developing countries' food systems. This review is part of the background against which policy options for the future must be examined.

Two major areas of concern will be highlighted below, urbanisation and rural-urban relationships on the one hand, and access to resources and implications of technological change on the other. Structural change in these areas has important implications for developing countries' food systems in terms of food production and consumption, with regard to both the overall situation and the impact on specific groups of producers and consumers.

1.   URBANISATION AND RURAL-URBAN RELATIONSHIPS

The way in which urbanisation and rural-urban relationships affect the domestic food system can range from very adverse effects (as explained by the proponents of the theory of economic and social dualism) to a situation of mutual support. It all depends on how the underlying forces and mechanisms operate (with a more or less strong role of government) in the use of rural resources and the distribution of the benefits thereof.

While the model of a dual economy tends increasingly to be rejected because it "presents an inaccurate and to some extent misleading picture" and exaggerates exploitative relationships, it seems that the concept still retains "a good deal of meaning" (1), in particular in some African countries. For this reason, and because it lends itself well to the illustration of certain mechanisms, we shall refer to the concept of dualism in the following section. But we shall also offer suggestions for overcoming dualism and establishing mutually-beneficial rural-urban relations.

The "modern dual economy" has been described by Murdoch (2) as consisting of a modern urban sector supported by an urban power elite (possibly including absentee landlords) and a stagnant rural sector where the majority of the population is maintained in a marginal existence. Another characteristic of the modern sector (which can include cash crop production for export) is its outward orientation. This is reflected in a "modern export enclave economy" to which import substitution activities are gradually added (3). How is the food system affected by dual economies? This question can be seen on three levels: first with regard to food production, second with regard to the demand for food, and third, and more indirectly, in terms of the effects on resource allocation.

Neglect of the traditional rural sector, where food production tends to be located, depresses food supply through several mechanisms: the physical base of production is weakened by allocating more and better land to export crops or non-agricultural uses (e.g. urban sprawl) (4); producers are induced to migrate to urban areas (pulled by the attractions of urban life and/or pushed by the expansion of modern enclave agriculture); the economic incentive for surplus food production is kept low since the powerful urban sector (both private and public) presses for low consumer prices to help export industries and for government to keep wages down. This economic disincentive effect prevents modernisation and intensification of food production and may be exacerbated by poor infrastructure which makes for high transport costs and lower farm gate prices than would otherwise be possible. Another disincentive effect may lie in the orientation of the modern manufacturing sector (producing non-essential consumer goods for the urban market or for export) which does not offer sufficient goods in demand by agricultural producers, who will therefore restrain their market production.

Thus the squeezing of traditional agriculture and its weak links with the rest of the economy tend to keep food production low and domestic resources under-utilised. However, this may not apply throughout the agricultural sector. The modern sector's need for cheap food has sometimes (e.g. Zambia) favoured food production on modern commercial farms which may be more competitive than traditional farms, due to the use of modern technology and certain economies of scale in marketing and management. Even increasing food needs of urban areas may be met in such a way while maintaining the dual economy. The possible consequence of this kind of development, however, cannot be perceived in aggregate statistics of agricultural production. The gap between the modern and the traditional sectors will be widened by denying the peasant farmers a chance to sell (or sell more) to the modern sector. Peasant producers will remain trapped in their traditional sector, unable to modernise and intensify their production due to lack of demand and cash income.

This illustrates a characteristic of the dual economy, viz. its tendency to perpetuate itself and, in so doing, to reinforce the dichotomy between the two sectors. While possibly assuring increased food production more efficiently (at least in the short run), the development of a food production enclave in the modern sector is likely to have negative effects in terms of equity, in particular if people in the traditional sector have no alternative employment possibilities in the modern sector. Even where such possibilities exist, negative social effects cannot be excluded, for example in cases where a very low level of wages in the modern sector (be it plantation agriculture or manufacturing) is maintained thanks to a continuous flow of labourers from the traditional sector. This kind of pressure on the labour market can result in the inability of labourers to buy sufficient food for themselves in a situation where self-provisioning is no longer possible because the people have migrated to urban areas.

Thus, the dualistic structure and functioning of an economy can adversely affect the food system from both the supply and demand sides. In addition to the fact that the poorer section of the urban population lacks purchasing power to satisfy its food needs, the nature of food demand by the wealthier urban dwellers tends to put food imports in a favourable position (5). This is the case where the food consumption patterns of industrialised countries are emulated, including food products not produced domestically. Furthermore, urban consumers often prefer processed food items for their convenience. Processing of traditional food is usually not well developed and imports (either of the raw material or of final products) again win over domestic production. This tendency can be accentuated by poor infrastructure in the areas of transport, communications and hygiene which make imports more reliable, safer in health terms and at times even cheaper than comparable domestic products. Finally, when the dualistic economic structure has exerted its weakening influence on traditional agriculture over a long period, domestic capacity to meet the food requirements of a growing urban population will fall short of the increasing volume of demand. Food imports will then become a necessity for reasons not only of quality, but also of quantity of demand. This has important implications for food security, in particular in urban areas, which have been described as living "from ship to mouth" (6) in periods of world market scarcity.

In addition to the direct effects of dual economic structures on food production and demand, some more indirect effects have to be considered. While the immediate disincentive effect on food production of low producer prices has already been mentioned, dual economies are also characterised by other price distortions which, in a more indirect fashion, represent a burden for the traditional food sector, together with an urban bias in resource allocation. First, import substitution policies combined with industrial protection tend to put the prices of manufactures at higher levels than they would be otherwise, thus worsening the internal terms of trade for agriculture. Second, an overvalued currency favours imports of capital goods which are mainly used in the modern sector. Third, the price of credit may be distorted by interest subsidies, but loans are granted mostly to the modern sector. Fourth, minimum wage legislation fixing urban wages above the equilibrium level will, on the one hand, create a group of privileged urban wage earners and, on the other hand, increase the number of unemployed and underemployed (in particular recent migrants) who are often still supported by the rural community they left (7). Fifth, food subsidies tend to be limited to urban areas. This form of discrimination in public resource allocation frequently has its equivalent in the regional pattern of public investment and government spending on social services. Thus, while the transfer of resources from the rural to the urban sector can take many forms, rural areas are generally neglected when it comes to public spending. This is most striking when urbanisation is very rapid and demands an even higher share of public resources.

Urbanisation is a phenomenon which fits into the dichotomy of economic dualism. This is particularly true for the concept of "urban bias" developed by Michael Lipton and identified in both urban and rural development. But urbanisation also exists and has been analysed independently of the condition of dualism. The rapid growth and sheer volume of urban populations in developing countries, reinforced by rural-urban migration, and urban poverty, have been among the major concerns of analysis with a direct bearing on the food system.

Table 17 gives an idea of the magnitude and speed of urban population growth in developing countries, where more than two billion people are expected to live in urban areas by the year 2000. This is nearly five times the number in 1960 and nearly double the expected size of the urban population of developed countries, although the share of the urban population in the latter will reach 80 per cent, as against 41 per cent in developing countries.

Strong urban growth has been experienced in many developing countries, and rural-urban migration is perceived by most governments as a phenomenon to contain. Among 116 developing countries covered in a recent UN survey, 90 wanted to slow down or reverse rural-urban migration (8) but very few have actually been successful in doing so. Simmons reports (9) that China, Cuba and Malaysia are the only countries which have managed to slow metropolitan growth through agricultural development and regional planning. It is noteworthy that indirect measures of control such as employment creation, housing policy and food rationing systems have proved more effective than the direct prohibition of migration.

Lipton argues that the rate of urbanisation is often exaggerated because the different components of urban growth are not clearly distinguished (10). They are a) natural increase of initial urban populations, b) net immigration, c) natural increase of the new immigrants and d) "graduation" or boundary expansion that causes new communities to be counted as urban. Furthermore, international comparisons are misleading because the limit above which settlements are counted as towns are not the same in different regions of the world. Thus it may well be that exaggerated data are projected into the future. This suggests caution in dealing with data on urbanisation but does not affect the general implications of urbanisation for food systems which we propose to review.

There is evidence from a number of countries showing that per capita calorie availability in urban areas tends to be lower than in rural areas (11). For the urban dwellers of the lowest-income groups, this difference is particularly serious, amounting to 300-400 calories and bringing them close to or below the minimum nutritional level. Among the urban poor, recent immigrants from rural areas are especially vulnerable since they no longer have access to food produced in the household for direct consumption or available in a rural setting outside the cash economy.

Many studies have identified poverty as the main causal factor in malnutrition (12), although this can also depend heavily on environmental conditions and the functioning of the food system. Thus, in a study carried out in India (13), poor sanitation (associated with poverty) was seen to have played a greater part in childhood malnutrition than food intake. In this context, the decline of breastfeeding in urban areas has contributed to child malnutrition in low-income groups. Both the proportion of mothers who breastfeed and the duration of breastfeeding have declined as a result of increasing wage employment of urban mothers, the promotion of breast-milk substitutes and the social pressure for bottlefeeding as a status symbol. Poverty, poor hygienic conditions and inadequate child-care facilities (e.g. infants being

95

Table 17

URBAN POPULATION AND ITS ANNUAL GROWTH RATE (1) IN MAJOR REGIONS 1950-2000
(Millions and per cent)

	1950	1960	1970	1975	1980	1990	2000
World Total	724	1 012	1 354	1 561	1 807	2 422	3 208
%	3.35	2.91	2.84	2.93	2.92	2.81	
More developed regions	449	573	703	767	834	969	1 092
%	2.44	2.05	1.75	1.68	1.50	1.20	
Less developed regions	275	439	651	794	972	1 453	2 116
%	4.68	3.94	3.95	4.06	4.02	3.76	
Africa	32	50	80	103	133	219	346
%	4.42	4.85	4.97	5.10	5.00	4.56	
Latin America	68	107	162	198	241	343	466
%	4.57	4.21	4.01	3.86	3.56	3.06	
Northern America	106	133	159	171	183	212	239
%	2.29	1.80	1.33	1.45	1.47	1.19	
East Asia (including Japan)	113	195	265	309	359	476	622
%	5.46	3.09	3.06	3.03	2.82	2.67	
South Asia	105	147	217	266	330	516	791
%	3.37	3.91	4.01	4.33	4.47	4.27	
Europe	223	266	318	344	369	423	477
%	1.78	1.80	1.52	1.45	1.36	1.19	
Oceania	8	10	14	16	18	23	27
%	3.00	2.70	2.67	2.63	2.37	1.87	
USSR	71	105	138	155	174	209	240
%	3.91	2.75	2.42	2.23	1.87	1.35	

1.   Rounded figures, growth rates are annual averages pertaining to the
     decade (respectively 5-year period) starting with the year indicated.
     Therefore, no growth rates are given for the last column.

Source: Based on United Nations, Patterns of Urban and Rural Population
          Growth, Population Studies Series, No. 68, New York, 1980, Tables 4
          and 5.

looked after by older children) all contribute to dangerous practices of bottlefeeding which result in a high prevalence of diarrhea and infections (14).

Before elaborating on how and where poverty is created in the process of urbanisation and what remedial action could be taken, it is worth mentioning other nutritional implications of urbanisation which are not linked to poverty. These relate to the quality of food available and food habits. The substitution of nutritionally-inferior products for traditional foods is a frequently-mentioned phenomenon adversely affecting urban dwellers. One example is the "increasing consumption of white bread, generally of very low extraction flour [which] is likely to lead to vitamin B deficiencies" (15). However, the disruption of traditional diets by urban living conditions does not necessarily have only negative effects. The increasing diversity of food consumed is "sometimes for good, sometimes for ill" (16). Contrary to what seems to be the case in Peru and other Latin American countries, Austin further states that recent migrants tend to cling to traditional foods even if they are relatively expensive. Thus, stability of food habits can exacerbate the precarious economic situation of new urbanites.

This brings us back to the underlying issue of poverty which is explained by increasing inequalities, both intra-rural and rural-urban, caused by urbanisation (17). While it could be argued, somewhat mechanically, that rural-urban migration should leave those who stay behind better off because they have more land per capita, the reality is different in most cases due to the power relationships within the village and the fact that migration tends to affect the various groups of villagers differently (18).

The very poorest rural dwellers, i.e. subsistence farmers and landless labourers, tend also to be the least educated. Therefore they find it most difficult to leave the countryside. The wealthiest villagers, at the other end, have no incentive to give up their privileged position in order to migrate. Thus it is largely people from the middle strata, i.e. small landowners who used to produce some marketable surplus, who are attracted to urban areas. Migration therefore increases intra-rural inequality ipso facto. Inequality is further increased by the tendency of the richer villagers to take over the land of those who have left, thus strengthening their position as oligopolistic employers of agricultural labour. In the worst case, increasing farm size will make the introduction of labour-saving technology profitable with the consequence that some of the poorest villagers will eventually be forced to migrate. Thus, while better-off migrants are "pulled" out of the rural areas by the attractions of the town, the worst-off are "pushed" out by rural poverty and labour-replacing technology. The extent to which food output is affected in this process is an empirical question to be examined case by case. It is obvious, however, that this kind of structural change may imply reduced access to food for the poorer sections of the population. On the other hand, rural change and modernisation may also help to increase food availability and accessibility for the poor through increased production and lower prices, on the condition that they do not suffer a loss or reduction of their resource base due to the structural change in question (19).

The increase in rural-urban inequalities is partly a direct consequence of migration, since the sheer number and political weight of the increasing urban population (witness the occasional outbreak of urban unrest in various countries) leads to the allocation of an ever-growing proportion of resources to urban areas, thus leaving a dwindling share for rural areas and continuing the vicious circle of migration and poverty. Finally, the growing number of newcomers in urban areas, many of whom are unskilled and unable to find employment, will increase intra-urban inequality. To the extent that recent migrants are still supported by their villages, this adds to the burden shouldered by rural people. However, growing inequalities may be acceptable if they represent the price to be paid for a general increase in the living standards of most poor people.

2. REDUCING URBAN BIAS (20)

Since urbanisation poses problems for food systems in many poor countries, ways and means have to be found to overcome them. Making migration illegal, the most radical course of action for stopping urbanisation, has been shown to be ineffective in a number of countries; even if it were effective, it could only tackle the symptoms of the problem, not its deeper causes. Furthermore, it has to be recognised that, in a wider perspective, urbanisation is quite naturally associated with the development process. As such, it has to be accepted to a certain degree. However, policies have to be designed to relieve the undesired effects directly and "above all to decrease rural-urban and intra-rural inequality, especially to the extent that such inequality is also inefficient" (21).

In general terms, the "artificial disadvantages of rural life and agricultural activity" (22) should be removed. This concerns the supply of public services and infrastructure, together with the creation of widely accessible possibilities for improved income. Decentralising industry, in particular the part of industry placed upstream or downstream of the agricultural sector, and, where appropriate, introducing more labour-intensive technologies may be part of such a strategy (23). In such a context, agriculture and industry can be mutually stimulating, in particular when inter-sectoral terms of trade are perceived as being fair and the level of employment can be raised (24). The lack of effective demand for food by the urban poor can thus be overcome. Increasing incomes in urban areas will also change the structure of demand for food. Demand for higher quality and more varied food (e.g. milk, eggs, vegetables, fruit and meat) is more income elastic than staple food demand and will therefore increase more rapidly. Provided the necessary inputs are available and production of these food items can be organised in a labour-intensive fashion, this structural change offers scope for increased employment.

It would be misleading to assume, however, that the artificial disadvantages facing rural areas could be removed instantaneously and without resistance from those who benefit from the situation of inequality. Although it may reflect a very short-sighted perception of self-interest, such resistance has to be expected. In the longer run, the privileged could gain from accepting a more equitable access to resources now, since this may be necessary to engender the dynamic process of development alluded to above.

Some see in the resistance of privileged groups a deadlock which can only be overcome by revolution. Lipton (25) less categorically suggests that "substantial reduction of urban bias by 'peaceful persuasion' alone is not likely in many poor countries" but he does not deny that there is scope for improvement without revolution in most countries.

To the extent that politicians are not a monolithic group, are not exclusively influenced by class or other group pressure and are enlightened enough to see their long-run self-interest in equity, growth and development, they can play a role in reducing urban bias. Given the usual power relationships, this is a very delicate course of action and may require "indirect or half-hidden shifts of resources and prices" (26) in favour of the rural sector, rather than an open confrontation with urban interests. A change in life-style by the elite (e.g. following the Gandhian idea of occasional free work in the countryside) could help further to reduce the alienation of rich urbanites from the rural poor.

The change in policies and attitudes would also have to be reflected in organisational changes in the public services which traditionally embody urban bias in their way of functioning. Where traditional relations have destroyed confidence between government and rural people, this needs to be restored.

In addition to policies of more balanced resource allocation (including price policies), the following policies to reduce urban bias and its adverse effects on developing countries' food systems might be considered:

-- Emphasis on calorie-efficient crops consumed by the rural poor;

-- Better access to education pari passu with skilled employment possibilities in rural areas;

-- Efforts to spread knowledge about urban/rural inequality to help government give greater emphasis to rural areas;

-- More applied agricultural research linked to rural development, with emphasis on smallholdings, poor man's crops and appropriate technology.

National policies and attitudes are generally dominant in both the creation and possible reduction of urban bias. Foreign aid agencies can play a role in supporting such policies but can hardly be expected successfully to counteract national policies. Therefore, where governments are not fully committed to reducing urban bias, attempts to do so by foreign assistance are unlikely to succeed in more than a very limited way. On the other hand, given the subtlety of urban bias in many instances, the design and implementation of projects to reduce it, even in a favourable environment, require the representatives of donor agencies to be intimately acquainted with specific field conditions and rural communities. It further implies decentralisation of experts, control and cash.

3. ACCESS TO RESOURCES AND IMPLICATIONS OF TECHNOLOGICAL CHANGE

The extent and way in which people have access to resources largely determines their access to food and, together with environmental factors, their nutritional situation. Access to land and the degree of malnutrition are linked, as has been shown, for example, by studies in the Indian State of Punjab, Bangladesh, Guatemala and Costa Rica (27). If structural change reduces access to land, there is thus a high risk that malnutrition will be increased simultaneously.

Clay (28) sees the rural poor in three categories according to their access to and control over production assets. First there are the rural landless; their proportion in total rural population is particularly high in Bangladesh and North-East India (30-40 per cent). They are in the weakest position of all the rural groups since they depend on wage income from (often unstable) employment. Their real income can be adversely affected in two ways at the same time: as a consequence of crop failure, employment opportunities are likely to be reduced, and food prices tend to rise (29). Second, in a slightly less vulnerable situation, are the near-subsistence households. The third category is composed of poor small farmers producing marketable surpluses.

Clearly defined seasonal and regional dimensions of poverty and malnutrition affecting different social groups have been shown in the studies on Zambia, Bangladesh and India reviewed by Clay (30). They can be exacerbated by environmental stress (31) and population pressure, both of which tend to reduce access to land. The latter is particularly severe in Asia. The indebtedness of poor farmers is another mechanism -- possibly linked to population pressure and environmental stress -- of losing access to land. The cycle may start out with a poor harvest or some other calamity. Debts are contracted to tide over the difficult period. But due to high interest rates, and/or the obligation to sell the subsequent harvest on unfavourable terms, it is very difficult for a poor farmer to overcome his indebtedness without, in the end, selling part or all of his land. Thus different forces may combine to reduce access to land of the rural poor.

But access to land is not sufficient to assure an adequate food supply for those holding the land. Complementary production factors such as water, seeds and fertilizers and the necessary finance to procure these factors are of increasing importance in the context of modern agriculture. Where the structures of wealth and power relationships limit the access of small farmers to these resources (32), food availability for these groups is reduced. If there were sufficient employment opportunities outside agriculture, producers constrained in this way might take them and obtain access to food by exercising their "effective demand" backed up by non-agricultural income. However, the structure of many developing economies is often such that both effective demand and access to productive resources severely limit access to food.

Special provisions giving the poor more equal access to resources would be one way of improving the situation. Land reform and land tenure might also be considered. These issues are closely related to the power structure of any given society and will be dealt with below. Other less fundamental but nevertheless essential issues are implied in government policies aiming to support agriculture. It is claimed that small farmers deserve special attention not only for reasons of equity but also because of their "dynamic efficiency" (33). It is by now widely accepted that small farmers in most developing countries are more efficient producers than larger farmers (34). But even if private estates and state farms pass the test of static economic efficiency, so Acharya's argument goes, they should not be promoted because their benefits are likely to be much less widely distributed than those from smallholder production of the same output. As a consequence, "estate farms are less likely to set in motion the broad-based increases in rural purchasing power that are necessary to bring about a mutually supportive dynamic interaction between agriculture and domestic industry" (35).

a) Productivity and farm size

Countries aiming above all to increase their agricultural production may be tempted to favour large farms on the assumption that there are certain economies of scale in farm management (e.g. in obtaining and applying inputs, credit and advice). It also appears easier to deal with a smaller number of producers to meet, for example, the food needs of a given area. However, there is evidence that small farmers tend to make more intensive use of land and labour and therefore show higher output per land area available.

Comparing land-use intensity of small and large farms on the basis of agricultural census data for 30 developing countries, Berry and Cline (36) found that "in practically all of these countries, the large farm sector (with the top 40 per cent of land area) uses its land less intensively than the small farm sector (with the bottom 20 per cent of the area)". This pattern is the stronger the more unequal the distribution of land. The hypothesis of a dual labour market, with cheap family labour working on small farms and more expensive wage labour on the larger farms may thus be confirmed. Furthermore, it has been shown for another set of 40 countries that farm output and employment per area of land tend to be higher in countries with smaller average farm size and more equal distribution of land.

More in-depth analysis by Berry and Cline in six countries (Brazil, Colombia, the Philippines, Pakistan, India and Malaysia) has confirmed the negative relationship between farm size and output per area of land available, even when allowance was made for differences in land quality (37). The same pattern has been found when output per acre was replaced by total social factor productivity, except for the very smallest farm sizes. It should be noted that higher productivity of small farms does not normally result from higher yields of specific crops but from more intensive land utilisation (multiple cropping).

However, as a country develops and non-farm employment opportunities increase (leading to a relatively high opportunity cost for labour), the superior productivity of small farms tends to fade away, as Berry and Cline found in the case of Japan. Similarly, the inverse relationship between farm size and land productivity can be weakened or eliminated by technological change (38), such as the introduction of High Yielding Varieties (HYV) on which we shall elaborate below after having briefly addressed the issues of land reform and land tenure.

b) Land reform and land tenure

The productive superiority of small farmers mentioned above would seem to suggest that land reform could be an important way of increasing food production in developing countries. Whether this suggestion is feasible for a given country depends first on the prevailing socio-political situation. There must be a strong political basis for the implementation of any land reform since it implies a change in power relationships. If one assumes that this condition is fulfilled, one has to ask what effects land reform can be expected to have on production. This question has to be seen both for the short and for the medium and long term. In the short term it would seem normal that the disruption of the production system should have negative rather than positive effects on output, and this is confirmed by a number of cases. But in the longer term there is evidence that, in many instances, land reform leads to increased production (39). However, land reform literature tends to refer to agricultural output in general rather than to food production (40). Similarly, it is striking that the 17 "Guiding Principles" adopted by the 1979 World Conference on Agrarian Reform and Rural Development do not mention the food issue explicitly (41). Nevertheless, it may be safe to assume that overall food production has increased in most cases where agricultural output grew after the implementation of land reform measures.

The direct beneficiaries of land reform are not necessarily the poorest, nor a majority of the rural population. Thus it has been argued that partial land reforms in Latin America have actually increased inequality in the rural population (42).

While historical experiences with land reform cannot provide models for other countries, and results cannot be expected to be necessarily similar in different countries, the literature seems to suggest that a number of conditions should be fulfilled in order to avoid a negative impact of land reform on output. For example, periods of uncertainty should be avoided and implementation of land reform measures should be swift. Furthermore, adequate services and infrastructure have to be provided to the beneficiaries of the land reform so that they can effectively make use of their new resources (43). This is particularly important where such services have previously been supplied by the landlords. Finally, the economic environment (e.g. market outlets and prices) and administrative modalities have to be such as to motivate the new land-owners to make full use of their new resources. In this context it has been suggested that administrative devolution and organization of the poor enhance the success of land reforms in terms of output and equity (44).

In the case of the Ivory Coast, where family farms with average land holdings of between two and three hectares dominate, Sawadogo (45) suggests that land reform should be seen as a question of increasing holdings by bringing idle or underutilised land under cultivation. This suggestion may also apply to other land-rich countries and to countries where, although land is scarce (e.g. Korea), productivity is constrained by the small size of farms which hinders modernisation (46).

Land ownership is not the only way of providing direct access to land resources. While tenancy and share-cropping are often seen as constituting disincentives to production (and thus an obstacle to productive superiority of small farmers), because tenants will not reap the full benefits resulting from additional inputs, they may still assure a more intensive use of the land than direct cultivation by larger farmers. Thus legislation limiting tenancy in a situation where proper land reform is not possible for political reasons may lead to the eviction of tenants and actually reduce access to land for the poorer members of rural society. In such situations, tenancy must be considered as second best, and rather than limiting it, government policy should aim at improving tenancy conditions and providing services to tenants. In addition, measures may be taken to facilitate land purchase by the tenants, e.g. provision of loans and progressive land taxation (47).

c) Implications of technological change

It is not the intention to examine here the whole spectrum of questions linked with technological change in agriculture but rather to concentrate on the implications of technological change for rural populations' access to resources and, by extension, to food. Three types of question are discussed in the literature, mainly with regard to "green revolution technology" (improved seeds, chemicals and water control) and mechanisation. The first question is whether small farmers can and actually do benefit from the new technology? Second, to what extent does technological change replace labour or raise labour requirements? Third, what impact can be expected on production costs and consumer prices?

One aspect of the first question is that of the new technology's "scale neutrality" in a purely technical sense. It seems to be generally recognized that the yield increasing (HYV) technology "can be used at least as efficiently on small as on large farms" (48). The other aspect, viz. that of effective access to an appropriate package of HYV technology, is more controversial. There is evidence that actual availability of certain inputs, in particular fertilizers and control of irrigation water, tends to be greater for larger farmers (49). On the other hand, small farmers tend to benefit from more motivated and cheaper labour (family labour) than larger farmers. Thus, reviewing research on HYV in Asia, Pearse found examples of small-holdings with both higher and lower yields than bigger holdings. Where the latter had invested heavily in operating capital and engaged in more careful and intensified husbandry, their yields tended to be superior. "An attempt to establish an overall relationship between yield per unit of land and size of holding under HYVs came to a somewhat indecisive conclusion" (50). This conclusion seems compatible with that drawn by S.S. Bhalla on the basis of nationwide survey data on India. He found that "the inverse relationship was still significant during the Green Revolution years of 1968-69 to 1970-71, though there was a moderate tendency for this relationship to weaken over time" (51).

Pearse identifies land-and-water improvement as the crucial element in increasing food supplies. If such an improvement can be achieved by mobilising the labour of the rural population and by using local materials, he sees prospects for small producers to share more fully the benefits of the new technology. Further conditions mentioned are the availability of fertilizer at acceptable cost, and appropriate mechanisation.

While it is acknowledged that HYVs are well suited to increase the income of small farmers and landless labourers because they raise labour requirements per acre, this potential can be perverted by the introduction of labour-saving mechanisation.

The use of tractors may be important in terms of timeliness of cultivation but it is also "the most discussed instance of employment destruction by machinery with, in many cases, a low or even negative social rate of return over cost" (52). Reviewing the experience of sub-Saharan Africa with tractorisation, Acharya concludes that it has been, "on balance, adverse ... and, in contrast with biologically-based innovations, ... typically labour-displacing". In many cases, problems of organisation, maintenance and inefficient use make tractorisation not only socially undesirable but also economically wasteful and inferior to cultivation by animal traction (53).

Especially where they are subsidised, tractors may, of course, improve the profitability of larger farms which can use them more economically than smaller farms. Hand tractors may offer a better chance for smaller farmers to benefit from mechanisation. Like other tractors, they may even increase employment where they are essential for the introduction of double cropping. However, the impact of tractorisation on cropping intensity has been found to be weak; in addition, it does not offset the employment losses in main-season ploughing. There is also evidence from Pakistan showing that "purchasers of large tractors over the last decade have tended both to expand the area they cultivate and to decrease the number of share-tenants on their land" (54). Even if agricultural output is increased in this process, access to food may be reduced for those who are evicted and cannot find adequate alternative sources of income.

The third question, viz. the impact of technological change on production costs and consumer prices, is addressed in the literature less explicitly than the preceding issues. While it requires more operating capital for inputs than traditional technology, HYV technology is economically efficient and thus causes unit production costs to decline. In theoretical terms, this can be expressed as a shift of the supply curve to the right, resulting in a lower equilibrium price. However, if larger farmers have benefitted more fully from the potential of HYVs, they may also be able to accept prices below the production costs of smaller farmers. Increased yields may push prices down to the level at which smaller farmers will have to increase their indebtedness or be forced out of the market and possibly off the land. Thus technical and economic progress is not tantamount to offering everybody a better deal but can, in an environment of marked inequality, increase that inequality and make disadvantaged groups of producers worse off than they were before. Consumers would be among the beneficiaries of such a scenario, however, and this might explain why it would probably appeal to many (urban-based) governments despite the longer-term negative effects of "urban bias" referred to in an earlier section.

To avoid reduced access to resources as a consequence of technological change, ways and means have to be found to allow the poorer groups of the population to benefit from technological change more fully. Lipton suggests three general principles which seem appropriate in this context (55). First, technologies embodying diseconomies of scale should be developed, e.g. improvement of small-scale grain storage systems which cannot profitably be seized by the rich. Second, technologies complementary to labour should be promoted so as to secure employment and the benefits of divisibility, e.g. hand pumps in Bangladesh. Third, those threatened with displacement by labour-saving innovations which are economic at any plausible set of prices should become co-operative owners of the capital goods embodying such innovations, e.g. huller mills.

NOTES AND REFERENCES

1. I. Livingstone and H.W. Ord, Agricultural Economics for Tropical Africa, Heinemann, London, 1981, pp. 39-40.

2. W.W. Murdoch, The Poverty of Nations -- The Political Economy of Hunger and Population, Johns Hopkins University Press, Baltimore, 1980.

3. Murdoch notes that China, Taiwan and South Korea have largely avoided the dual economy trap. He sees the export enclave economy as typical of Africa and of some Asian countries (Bangladesh, Burma, Sri Lanka). Other Asian countries, e.g. India, Indonesia, Pakistan and the Philippines, and Latin America are given as examples of import substitution economies. See W.W. Murdoch, op. cit., pp. 235-237.

4. For example, it has been reported that 26 000 ha are lost annually to urban sprawl in Egypt; see K. Newland, "City Limits: Emerging Constraints on Urban Growth", Worldwatch Paper No. 38, Washington, D.C., 1980, p. 13.

5. For this and other demand effects, see K. Vergopoulos, "l'Agriculture périphérique dans le Nouvel Ordre International, Refléxions sur la question des systèmes alimentaires nationaux", in Revue Tiers Monde, Vol. XXII, No. 85, 1981.

6. K. Newland, op. cit., p. 12.

7. See K. Campbell, "The Effects of Urbanisation on Agriculture", in D. Ensminger (ed.), Food Enough or Starvation for Millions, McGraw-Hill, New Delhi, 1977, who argues that such transfers in support of migrants tend to be higher than remittances from urban to rural areas. Lipton, however, refers to research done in 10 villages in Southern India where a rough balance of the two flows was found; see M. Lipton Why Poor People Stay Poor, A Study of Urban Bias in World Development, Temple Smith, London, 1977, P. 236.

8. UN/ECOSOC, Population Commission, 20th Session, "Concise Report on Monitoring of Population Policies", E/CN.9/338, 1978.

9. A.B. Simmons, "A Review and Evaluation of Attempts to Constrain Migration to Selected Urban Centres and Regions", in UN, Population Distribution Policies in Development Planning, Population Studies Series, No. 75, New York, 1981, p. 95.

10. M. Lipton (1977), op. cit., p. 216. Lipton makes this distinction very clear in a paper delivered at the 12th IIDC Conference in Ottawa, October 1981, entitled "Rural Development and the Retention of the Rural Population in the Countryside of Developing Countries" (revised

version published in the <u>Canadian Journal of Development Studies</u>, Vol. 3, No. 1, 1982).

11. FAO, <u>The Fourth World Food Survey</u>, Rome, 1977, pp. 33-36, contains comparative data for India, Sri Lanka, Tunisia and certain regions of Brazil. However, prevalence of malnutrition has been claimed to be higher in rural and remote areas than in urban areas in Africa. This claim has been made on the basis of data from National Nutrition Surveys conducted in Egypt, Cameroon, Liberia, Togo and Sierra Leone. See S.K. Kumar, "Nutrition Concerns in Food Policy for Sub-Saharan Africa", in IFPRI, <u>Food Policy Issues and Concerns in Sub-Saharan Africa</u>, Washington, D.C., 1981.

12. See, for example, J.E. Austin, <u>Confronting Urban Malnutrition, The Design of Nutrition Programs</u>, Johns Hopkins University Press, London, 1980, World Bank Staff Occasional Paper No. 28.

13. FAO, (1977), <u>op. cit.</u>, p. 39.

14. <u>Ibid.</u>, p. 44, drawing also on data from Africa and Latin America; similarly, J.E. Austin, <u>op. cit.</u>, p. 38 comparing Bangkok and rural areas in Thailand with regard to breastfeeding. For a survey of trends in breastfeeding as revealed by 18 studies in different countries of Africa, Asia and Latin America, see J. Mayer and J.T. Dwyer, <u>Food and Nutrition Policy in a Changing World</u>, New York, Oxford University Press, 1979, Table 11-1.

15. F.T. Sai, "Food, Population and Politics", Occasional Essay No. 3, International Planned Parenthood Federation, London, 1977, p. 7.

16. J.E. Austin, <u>op. cit.</u>, p. 38.

17. See M. Lipton (1977), <u>op. cit.</u>, p. 221.

18. We rely here on M. Lipton, <u>ibid.</u>, who elaborates in more detail, pp. 216-237.

19. See below for further elaboration on the implications of technological change.

20. The prescriptions made in this section may appear overly optimistic. However, this optimism should not be interpreted to mean that changes will be easy to introduce, only that they are possible. There is evidence that governments succeed to some extent in reducing the urban bias in nutrition, for example in Papua New Guinea, Micronesia and Fiji; see J. Lambert, "The Effect of Urbanisation and Western Foods on Infant and Maternal Nutrition in the South Pacific", in <u>Food and Nutrition Bulletin</u>, Vol. 4, No. 3, July 1982, pp. 11-13.

21. M. Lipton (1981), <u>op. cit.</u>, p. 36.

22. M. Lipton (1977), <u>op. cit.</u>, p. 237.

23. See C.G. Baron (ed.), Technology, Employment and Basic Needs in Food Processing in Developing Countries, Pergamon Press, Oxford, 1980, for a wide range of examples of technological adjustment possibilities.

24. On the supporting role of industry in agricultural development, see S. Amin, "Pour une stratégie alternative du développement -- l'industrie au service de l'agriculture", in Afrique et Développement, Vol. VI, No. 3, 1981, pp. 116-125.

25. M. Lipton (1977) op. cit., p. 329; in a last chapter (pp. 328-352) with the title "What can be done?", Lipton discusses various possible courses of action on which we draw here. For a rather pessimistic view of the scope for improvement via either reform or revolution, see W.W. Murdoch, op. cit., pp. 313-315.

26. M. Lipton (1977), op. cit., p. 338.

27. See FAO, "Examen d'analyse de la réforme agraire et du développement rural dans les pays en voie de développement depuis le milieu des années soixante", CMRADR/INF 3, Rome 1979, p. 9.

28. E.J. Clay, "Food Policy Issues in Low Income Countries: An Overview", in World Bank Staff Working Paper No. 473, August 1981, pp. 1-19.

29. On the dilemma of food price policy for poor consumers on the one hand and production incentives on the other hand, see C.P. Timmer, "Food Prices and Food Policy Analysis in LDCs" in Food Policy, Vol. 5, No. 3, 1980, pp. 188-199. A very recent and comprehensive treatment of price policy is contained in G.S. Tolley et al., Agricultural Price Policies and the Developing Countries, Johns Hopkins University Press, 1982.

30. E.J. Clay, op. cit., p. 8.

31. See E.P. Eckholm, Losing Ground: Environmental Stress and World Food Prospects, Worldwatch Institute, Washington D.C., 1976.

32. See, for example, J.K. Boyce and B. Hartman, "Hunger in a Fertile Land", in Ceres, March-April 1981, pp. 32-35.

33. See S.N. Acharya, "Perspectives and Problems of Development in Sub-Saharan Africa", in World Development, Vol. 9, 1981, pp. 109-147.

34. For a very detailed and broadly based discussion of this issue on which we draw in the following section, see R.A. Berry and W.R. Cline, Agrarian Structure and Productivity in Developing Countries, Johns Hopkins University Press, Baltimore, 1979.

35. S.N. Acharya, op. cit., p. 131.

36. R.A. Berry and W.R. Cline op. cit., p. 40-43.

37. Ibid., p. 126.

38. See, for example, I. Ahmed, <u>Technological Change and Agrarian Struc-</u> <u>ture: A Study of Bangladesh</u>, ILO, Geneva, 1980; similarly V. Rao and T. Chotigeat, "The Inverse Relationship between Size of Holdings and Agricultural Productivity", in <u>American Journal of Agricultural Econ-</u> <u>omics</u>, August 1981, pp. 521-574.

39. For Latin America, see S. Eckstein et al., "Land Reform in Latin America: Bolivia, Chile, Mexico, Peru and Venezuela", World Bank Staff Working Paper No. 275, Washington D.C., 1978; for calculation of the potential effects of land redistribution on agricultural output in Brazil, Colombia, India, Pakistan, Philippines and Malaysia and a short review of experience in other countries, see R.A. Berry and W.R. Cline, <u>op. cit.</u>, pp. 131-140.

40. See, for example, M. Bezzabeh, "A Review of the Recent Trends in Agrarian Reform and Rural Development in Tropical Africa", in <u>Land</u> <u>Reform: Land Settlement and Cooperatives</u>, No. 1-2, FAO, Rome, 1981.

41. See FAO, "Conférence Mondiale sur la Réforme Agraire et le Développe- ment Rural", Rome 12-20 juillet 1979 Rapport (WCARRD/REP), pp. 2-4.

42. A. de Janvry and L. Ground, "Types and Consequences of Land Reform in Latin America", in <u>Latin American Perspectives</u> 19(1978): 96, referred to by W.W. Murdoch, <u>op. cit</u>,. p. 154.

43. There was a lack of such services during the land reform in Korea and apparently no production effects occurred during the five-year period following the reform; see Dong-Hi Kim and Yong-Jae Joo, <u>The Food</u> <u>Situation and Policies in the Republic of Korea</u>, OECD Development Centre, Paris, 1982, p. 49.

44. See K. Griffin and J. James, <u>The Transition to Egalitarian Development,</u> <u>Economic Policies for Structural Change in the Third World</u>, MacMillan Press, London, 1981, pp. 60-62.

45. A. Sawadogo, <u>L'Agriculture en Côte d'Ivoire</u>, Presses Universitaires de France, Paris, 1977, p. 221.

46. See Dong-Hi Kim and Yong-Jae Joo, <u>op. cit.</u>, p. 82.

47. See R.A. Berry and W.R. Cline, <u>op. cit.</u>, p. 137.

48. W.W. Murdoch, <u>op. cit.</u>, p. 145; see also B.H. Farmer (ed.), <u>Green</u> <u>Revolution?</u>, MacMillan, London, 1977.

49. See A. Pearse, <u>Seeds of Plenty, Seeds of Want, Social and Economic</u> <u>Implications of the Green Revolution</u>, Clarendon Press, Oxford, 1980.

50. <u>Ibid.</u>, pp. 107-108.

51. S.S. Bhalla, "Farm Size, Productivity, and Technical Change in Indian Agriculture", Appendix A in R.A. Berry and W.R. Cline, <u>op. cit.</u>, p. 184.

52.   M. Lipton, "Technological Cures for Social Pathologies", in The Journal of Development Studies, Vol. 15, No. 4, July 1979, p. 347.

53.   S.N. Acharya, op. cit., p. 133.

54.   R.A. Berry and W.R. Cline, op. cit., p. 139, making reference to J.P. McInerney and G.J. Donaldson, "The Consequences of Farm Tractors in Pakistan", World Bank Staff Working Paper No. 210, Washington D.C., 1975.

55.   See M Lipton (1979), op. cit., p. 348.

Chapter V

OUTLOOK

The aim of this final chapter is not to review recent global outlook reports which contain inter alia projections of demand and production for the year 2000 (1), but to highlight major issues and related policy options with which governments will be confronted in tackling food problems.

Even under optimistic assumptions, there are expected to be in the year 2000 as many as 260 million undernourished people living in 86 developing countries (2). This should give a sense of urgency to our review of policy options. However, we shall not suggest unique and easy solutions but analysis and action allowing for a differentiated approach, since producers, consumers and political actors are faced with a great variety of situations to which policies must be adapted.

1. FACING UP TO THE NEEDS

It has been shown in the chapter on imports (see also Tables 5 and 6) that developing countries have become increasingly unable to meet their food needs from their own food production and, as a group, have relied more and more on cereal imports. While situations among countries vary, only a few could increase production at a rate higher than population growth. In all Sahel countries reviewed, per capita production has declined. The response to this situation differs from country to country, even within the same ecological zone such as the Sahel. Imports have rarely fully substituted for domestic production shortfalls in the poorest countries. While the cereal imports of poor African countries do not amount to much in terms of world cereal trade, their importance is increasing compared to domestic production. On the other hand, better-off developing countries have considerably increased their share in world imports.

Projecting growth of staple crop production and consumption requirements for different groups of developing market economies and by region, IFPRI (3) found for all groups of countries and regions that consumption requirements will lie above the expected production level (see Table 18). Therefore, the tendency towards increasing imports is likely to continue. Countries which cannot afford to increase imports on commercial terms, or cannot obtain sufficient amounts of food aid, may be faced with declining per capita availability of food. This problem is most serious in the low-income countries, particularly in Africa. For that continent, FAO projects an annual per capita decline of food production of 0.4 per cent for the period 1980 to 2000 (4).

Table 18

ANNUAL GROWTH RATES OF STAPLE CROP PRODUCTION AND CONSUMPTION
REQUIREMENTS OF FOOD DEFICIT MARKET ECONOMIES

Country Categories	Projected Production Growth Rate 1975-1990	Required Production Growth Rates to Meet Consumption Requirements in 1990 (1)			
		At 1975 Per Capita Level	Low Income Growth	High Income Growth	At 110% of Energy Requirement
Low income	2.4	3.0	3.7	3.9	4.4
Middle income	3.5	3.7	4.3	4.5	3.9
High income	2.4	5.9	7.2	7.6	6.4
Total DME (2)	2.7	3.4	4.1	4.4	4.4
Regions					
Asia	2.5 (2.3)	3.1 (3.0)	3.7 (3.6)	4.0 (3.9)	4.3 (4.1)
North Africa/ Africa	2.5	4.2	4.9	4.4	4.6
Latin America	3.7 (3.6)	3.9 (2.6)	4.5 (3.2)	4.6 (3.3)	4.1 (.28)
Total DME (2)	2.7 (2.9)	3.4 (3.1)	4.1 (3.8)	4.4 (4.0)	4.4 (4.0)

1. Based on the trend value of production for 1975.
2. Developing market economies

N.B.: The figures in parentheses include the grain-exporting countries.

Source: IFPRI, Food Needs of Developing Countries, Research Report No. 3, Washington, D.C., December 1977, p.22.

Increased food production for domestic consumption is a necessary but not always sufficient condition to alleviate the problem in most poor countries. Lombard (5) has established three categories of countries in Africa which, though different, should all put emphasis on food production for domestic consumption:

1. Countries which are essentially agriculture-based and have few export opportunities;

2. Countries which rely heavily on the export of commercially-vulnerable crops such as groundnuts and palm oil;

3. Countries which have both an agricultural and an industrial base and which meet their food needs through the export of commercially-vulnerable industrial products such as textiles.

As examples, Lombard cites Mali, Upper Volta and Rwanda for the first category, Senegal and Benin for the second category, and Morocco for the third category.

a) A differentiated view of needs

While most of the discussion of food problems at the global and country level is conducted in terms of food supply and availability, this concept is unsatisfactory when it comes to the food situation of specific social groups and individuals. In an analysis of four famines in Ethiopia and Bangladesh (6), Sen shows that what really matters for the individual is "entitlement" to food and not food availability. Thus, in three out of the four famines analysed, food availability did not collapse but all the groups affected (defined as occupation groups) suffered entitlement losses. Entitlements are typically based on trade, production, employment and transfers.

Labour which is displaced in the process of agricultural modernisation and thus loses its entitlement (i.e. employment) may actually coexist with a situation of expanding food supply. On the other hand, where intensification of agriculture implies increased labour use, food supply and entitlements may increase simultaneously. The concept of entitlement thus provides a more complete indicator of people's food situation than that of supply and overall availability. Policies have to aim at guaranteeing food entitlements and not just food availability. Through their origin, changes in entitlements also point more directly to the underlying causes of hunger (7).

Accepting Sen's concept of food entitlement in the review of factors affecting food consumption and nutrition, Pinstrup Andersen suggests that consideration be given to two additional factors, namely consumption preferences of the head of household and the availability and prices of non-food commodities and services. "Improving food entitlement among households with members who are calorie-protein deficient need not result in significant reductions in such deficiencies. The improved entitlement may be utilised on food for well-nourished members of the household; it may be spent on food with low nutritional value, or it may be spent on non-foods" (8). Therefore, the analysis and policy prescriptions have to acknowledge the importance of authority structures and the division of labour within kinship groups and make the necessary differentiation (9).

Policies aiming at the satisfaction of the food needs of the weaker members of society will have to assure that their entitlements are maintained or increased. This can be done both on the production side and on the consumption side with food price policies as a central element affecting both of them.

On the production side, the question is who produces what, where and when, for own consumption or for market supply? This may reveal seasonal fluctuations of entitlements based on trade and/or production. Kumar (10) notes that food produced and stored at the household level provides a more continuous flow of income (real and monetary) than cash crops. Furthermore, the spending pattern of cash crop income tends to be different from that of food crop income, concentrating more on items requiring relatively large sums of money (clothing, education, consumer durables), thus possibly limiting access to food for certain members of the household. Consequently, production decisions and policies attempting to influence them should not be based exclusively on considerations of comparative economic advantage (neglecting distributional questions) but should also pay attention to nutritional implications.

This argument applies not only to the possible dichotomy between food crops and non-food crops but also to the selective support of food crops. Here the mechanisms involved are based on different consumption patterns of various groups of the population, different degrees of labour intensity in the production of various crops, and possibly a pattern of specialisation of farmers (by region, by farm size or resource availability). Production support activities, ranging from research and extension to input supply and price policies, could be targeted in such a way as to reflect the aim of satisfying nutritional needs. Such targeting may also be justified on the grounds that it mitigates distortions introduced earlier into the food system, e.g. past emphasis on promoting export crops and food crops preferred by urban consumers. Furthermore, selective policies will be more manageable in terms of their more limited resource requirements for implementation.

A related issue worth underlining is that of "low-risk" or "high-security" crops which can make an important contribution to attenuating fluctuations in food production (seasonal and year to year) and entitlements. Some traditional crops such as sorghum, millet and cassava, which survive better than many new varieties under climatic strain and low input levels, have been singled out as high-security crops (11). Since they may have lower yield potentials than "modern" crops, or are considered inferior to the latter, they have tended to be neglected throughout the food system. To make up for that neglect, and because of their high value in terms of food security, they deserve special support, for example in the form of increased research, extension and marketing efforts, provided there is consumer acceptance and there are longer-term economic prospects for such crops.

A different approach to the same concern about seasonal and year to year fluctuations is that of making modern varieties more resistant to environmental strain. The two approaches are not mutually exclusive and can theoretically be pursued simultaneously. However, due to budgetary constraints for research organisations, a choice may have to be made in certain cases. In this event, those traditional crops which are also inferior goods may deserve priority because they meet the food needs of the poorer sections of the population. But other factors would also have to be considered in such a decision, e.g. the labour intensity of the alternative crops and their capacity to maintain and increase food entitlements of large numbers of consumers.

Policies affecting food production will normally also affect consumption, for example via volume of supply and prices. Production policies may actually be designed with either producers or consumers (who are partly identical) in mind. They may also attempt to reconcile consumers' and producers' conflicting interests, for example by targeting special support (subsidies) to producers whose marketed surplus meets the needs of a target group of consumers at low price. Targeting is not only a way of meeting the needs of the most deprived people but it is also a device for keeping the overall cost low.

b) The role of price policies: output and distribution issues

Depending on the way in which price policies are used, they may favour either producers or consumers. But they may also be used to differentiate between various categories and -- possibly at high budgetary cost -- to satisfy both with a scheme of subsidisation which makes producer prices higher and consumer prices lower than they would be otherwise (12). In any case, price policies play a central role in all food systems.

Price policy is often the most important single short-term measure a government can take to influence the pattern of agricultural production and consequently of income distribution. But it is also an extremely difficult instrument to use judiciously because of the many ramifications of its effects and the great number of uncertainties concerning its impact (weather, and the reactions of producers, consumers and the production support and output delivery systems). In addition, food price policies have to be compatible with a country's relations with the outside world.

If imported food is cheaper than domestically-produced food, one has to ask whether and how domestic food producers should be protected against cheap imports or whether they should specialise in other crops or even move to other activities. Considerations of comparative advantage have to be accompanied by those of food security, social implications and practical feasibility. Industrialisation based on cheap labour may require low food prices for consumers to make industrial output prices competitive in the international market. On the other hand, imports of modern inputs for agriculture may increase productivity and reduce unit costs in food production. Thus the food price policy of a given country has to take into account existing and desirable relations with the international economy and their reconciliation with the internal requirements of development.

Prices of agricultural products, and in particular food crops, have frequently been kept below their market level, a practice which constitutes the most common disincentive to agricultural production. A study carried out by the US Department of Agriculture, covering 44 countries, found that such measures "were more widely used in South America and Asia than in Africa, in part reflecting the fact that many African economies are still largely on a subsistence basis" (13).

The increasing inability of many developing countries to cover the food requirements of their growing populations either domestically or through imports has enhanced the interest in price policies which would provide an incentive to production and at the same time make food available to consumers at reasonable prices. This implies increased attention to food production for domestic consumption, as opposed to export crops (food and non-food), and a careful analysis of the balance between production and consumption interests which have to be differentiated.

As a first step, the elimination of existing producer disincentives may "go a long way toward providing the right environment for the required acceleration of production" (14).

Governments have sometimes become deeply involved through price policies in the management of related activities in agriculture and other sectors of the economy. To what extent this is desirable in specific cases should be decided on grounds of efficiency and equity rather than ideology. In individual cases, it has been maintained recently that there was "excessive government interference" in agriculture (15).

The following review of objectives, instruments and achievements of price policies is intended to clarify the issues involved and thus to provide elements for more rational decision making. But it cannot develop any universally applicable guidelines.

Price Policies as Production Policies

The objective of increased food production, while generally appealing in times of shortage, can be challenged on the grounds of the comparative advantage a country or region may have in other crops or other activities. Furthermore, the objective, though easily receiving highest priority in policy statements, in fact competes with other objectives or is subject to constraints: for example, the need for fiscal and foreign exchange income which is frequently provided by non-food exports. If the comparative advantage of non-food crops can be established, a case against increased food production is made in terms of national income. But this could be outweighed by the desire to guarantee food entitlements. In the case of Senegal, for which Berg sees a comparative advantage in groundnuts, any "non-economic" expansion of food production (for reasons of food security) could be avoided by broadening the concept of self-sufficiency to include imports from neighbouring states (16). This assumes that the facilities for food distribution, both within the country and between neighbouring countries, actually exist and are adequate to cope with the change in the flows of agricultural products. Thus the argument based on economic advantage has to be checked against practical feasibility because distributional bottlenecks are often an important constraint even if imports would be economically advantageous.

In a similar vein, other objectives and constraints will affect the concrete formulation of food price policies. Inter alia, they will have to reflect the social implications of given food production objectives: who produces what and where? In other words, the production objectives have to take into account the problems of small farmers (and perhaps landless labourers), depressed regions and related cropping patterns.

If the production objectives are formulated with the necessary care and accepted, the question remains whether and to what extent price policies are an appropriate instrument by which to pursue these objectives. This issue has to be seen, on the one hand, in both the short and the long term and, on the other, in terms of aggregate and crop-specific supply response. The difference between the short term and the long term lies mainly in the possibility of introducing technological change.

With higher prices, aggregate supply in the short term (technology given) can increase only along the production function. Since immediately available resources tend to be fully utilised in poor countries, agriculture is "a sector of highly inelastic aggregate supply" under these assumptions (17). But even so, higher producer prices for specific crops may nevertheless lead to increased production where there is scope for switching from one crop to another. Thus, while agricultural price policy has frequently operated against food in the past (18), it should be possible to reverse this tendency. On a year-to-year basis, farmers can respond very markedly to price changes. But price policies relying on this kind of short-term response naturally face problems of timing, information and implementation.

While these policies may be vital at a given point in time, their development impact is low and can be negative at the margin. The longer-term supply response in a situation allowing for technological change, i.e. a shift in the production function, is more important. Higher prices may stimulate research (19), investment and the adoption of new technologies which increase not only the total production volume but productivity per acre, and reduce unit cost. This reaction requires time and a favourable environment. But it is now generally agreed that [with the exception of the very rare "perverse" response (20) or special rigidities] "the long-run aggregate supply elasticity for agriculture is greater than one, and that unfavourable farm prices have reduced significantly agricultural output and economic growth in many developing countries" (21).

Accepting, thus, that price incentives can be an effective tool to stimulate food production, one has to examine whether output prices should be supported or input prices subsidised. The immediate effect of both these tools is increased profitability, but they can have very different secondary effects and implications for food production. As ways of providing production incentives, however, they are not in principle mutually exclusive. In addition to the output impact, the all-pervasive income distribution effect has to be taken into account. A comparison between these two instruments would furthermore have to include the effects on investment, employment, government budgets and the balance of payments. While it is not practically meaningful to make such a comparison at a general level, comparisons have been made with regard to specific crops and countries. In the case of the Philippines, Barker and Hayami (22) conclude that fertilizer subsidies for rice production can have higher social returns per unit of government expenditure than can a support price above the import price of rice. In a short-term analysis of the case of Bangladesh, Ahmed (23) comes to a similar conclusion. However, both cases are too specific in their assumptions to provide a general argument in favour of subsidies.

While the more direct impact of input subsidies on the introduction of more productive technology seems to be widely accepted (24), there are also potential drawbacks. First, they cause a distortion in relative prices with a bias against additional employment and possibly in favour of imports. Second, especially if the subsidy is very large, it may encourage waste of the subsidised resource (e.g. water). Therefore, from the point of view of optimal allocation of resources, subsidies might better be phased out, once they have fulfilled their promotional role, if market prices can assure profitability.

Minimum support prices are used in many countries (25) and protect farmers against the risk of a sharp decline in market prices. They can, therefore, also facilitate the introduction of new technologies because farmers are protected against a price decrease below the minimum level resulting from increased production with new technology. Price stabilization between seasons has to be distinguished from inter-annual price stabilization. Both require a commitment and a capacity on the part of the government to buy and store (or to provide resources for these operations) at the desired price level. To function properly, the stabilization policy must also be credible. Otherwise, either it will not have the intended effect of encouraging producers, or speculation against the system may seem promising and will finally destabilize prices. For example, if traders believe that a given maximum price cannot be maintained at times of low crops, they can hold back and press for an increase in the stabilization level (26). Short-term stabilization needs basically the same administrative facilities as stabilization over several years. These facilities are often not available in developing countries, with the result that only partial stabilization is achieved and it is accompanied by negative income effects and perhaps physical losses. As for the amount of financial and physical resources required, inter-annual stabilization is much more demanding, since a series of either bumper crops or poor harvests will trigger off massive interventions. It may simply be too costly to be feasible (27). Moreover, if stabilization is effective at a fixed price or with a narrow price range between years, it can destabilize producer incomes. Thus, what may at first glance be considered as an effective instrument for the promotion of production is fraught with difficulties and possible adverse effects (28). Its use can only be recommended if greatest care is taken in its design and implementation, in analysing its possible implications case by case, and if the necessary resources can be made available.

Price Policies as Income Policies

Where food price policies have aimed at cheap supplies for urban consumers, the main preoccupation has been with the real income of consumers as a whole or of certain groups of consumers. However, it is now increasingly recognised that the income effect on producers deserves at least equal attention (29), irrespective of the original motivation of specific policies. We shall first briefly review the income effects of price policies designed to help the producers and then focus on the income effects of consumer-oriented price policies. In both cases, producers and consumers have to be considered separately.

Policies which increase or support producer prices benefit (in both absolute and relative terms) larger producers more than smaller producers, since the former have a higher share of marketable surplus. At the margin, very small farmers who are net purchasers of food (i.e. who produce well below their needs) may even incur a loss in income when food prices increase, whereas their real income would be protected by measures of price stabilisation. On the other hand, price stabilisation tends to maintain the income of bigger farmers better than that of small farmers whose marketable surplus fluctuates relatively more (30). Furthermore, larger farmers tend to be able to obtain more than a proportional share of subsidised inputs, both because of their personal relationships with the power elite and because they face fewer economic and administrative obstacles in securing and using subsidised credit and material inputs (31). This bias against the small farmer may be attenuated or avoided if the price support or input subsidy is limited to a food crop which is mainly or only produced by smaller farmers. However, to assure this result, effective measures have to be applied to prevent leakages.

As to consumers, it is also the poorest among them who will be relatively more affected by increasing food prices because of the bigger share of food in their expenditure pattern. This may mean reduced consumption for those who are already at a low level of intake. Furthermore, the change in the expenditure pattern of high-income groups due to increased food prices can, as a secondary effect, reduce employment. Mellor concludes for India that "the secondary effects... may contribute at least as much to depressing the real incomes of the poor as the direct effects of price on consumption" (32).

If the price increase concerns a food crop which is an inferior good for the poor, they will be hit even harder. Therefore, whenever possible, price policy should distinguish between preferred food (promote higher prices) and secondary grains and root crops. The latter may be subsidised to protect the poor (33).

Higher prices and input subsidies should be oriented and supported in such a way that productivity increases in the longer run, leading to higher production and lower unit prices which would still be remunerative and permit the satisfaction of low-income demand. To bridge the period needed to increase productivity massively, and in cases where this will not be sufficient to provide adequate food for everybody, countries may pursue or consider introducing directly consumer-oriented price policies, i.e. cheap food policies. These usually involve food imports, the implications of which have been dealt with in an earlier chapter of this report.

2. MAKING BETTER USE OF RESOURCES

Although there is scope for area expansion for agriculture, in particular in parts of Latin America and Africa, it seems to be generally agreed that the major contribution to additional crop production in the future has to come from research-based yield increases and more intensive cropping (34). Research into soils, water use, energy and genetic resources will have to play a major role in this process (35). Research is a necessary but not a sufficient condition for better use of resources. To achieve this, research results have to be effectively transmitted to farmers, who must be in a position to follow the advice given (36).

Better use of resources does not necessarily imply increased production. It could also be reflected in decreased post-harvest losses. This issue has received much attention since the UN General Assembly in 1975 called for a 50 per cent reduction in post-harvest losses. While not denying the importance of this subject, we shall not go into it here because of its technical nature and its recent treatment elsewhere (37).

The potential for yield increases becomes obvious if one compares average yields in developing countries with those achieved in the United States and elsewhere (see Table 19), without assuming, however, that yields could be the same in all countries.

a) Refocussing research

Because about 75 per cent of food is produced on rainfed lands, research should devote particular attention to these areas. The visibility of large irrigation schemes and their practical assurance against crop failures make them look very attractive. However "the very large investments devoted to irrigation have often led to disappointing results and in some cases to large areas eventually going out of production due mainly to waterlogging and salinity ... Various studies of rehabilitation versus new construction suggest that equivalent production increases could be achieved by rehabilitation with one-third the cost of new construction" (38).

For vast areas of irrigated and rainfed land, a package of cultivation practices which are within the capabilities of even small farmers of very limited means can improve substantially the levels and reliability of yields. "Timely planting with quality seeds of recommended varieties, at proper depths, adequate weed control and low-to-medium rates of recommended fertilization usually increase yields by about 100 per cent ... Research into ways and means of assisting and encouraging poor small farmers to apply such knowledge merits high priority" (39).

It is suggested that the initial emphasis should be placed on rainfed lands now under cultivation (40). Development of irrigation and new lands after very careful evaluation by soil scientists and other experts is proposed as a second element of the strategy. Finally, four other priorities deserve attention, but with great variations between environments and cultures:

1. Trees and their products;

2. Use of grazing lands;

3. Increased use of animal power;

4. Development or introduction of improved hand tools and animal-drawn machines.

This presentation of general approaches and priorities could give the impression that all the technologies are available and waiting to be applied. However, this is not always the case, in particular in Africa which Mellor compares in that respect with Asia in the late 1950s (41). The ease with which agricultural technology can be transferred across producing environments is often overestimated. It has been recognised that "international research centres alone are insufficient and that major technological gaps will remain ... unless national research capabilities can be improved and expanded" (42). To facilitate this task, the network of international institutes has been complemented by a new institution, the International Service for National Agricultural Research (ISNAR) which began operating in September 1980 in The Hague, Netherlands (43).

Table 19

SOME AVERAGE AND RECORD YIELDS IN TONS PER HECTARE, 1975 (1)

Crops	Average Yields t/ha (2)		
	Developing Countries	USA	World Record Yield
Maize	1.3	5.4	21.2
Wheat	1.3	2.1	14.5
Soybeans	1.5	1.9	7.4
Sorghum	0.9	3.3	21.5
Rice	-	2.5	14.4
Cassava	9.1	-	60.0

1. Adapted from Wortman and Cummings (1978).
2. National average yields for some developing countries are much lower.

Source: C.F. Bentley   et   al.,   "Enhancing   Agricultural   Production: Potentials, Constraints and Alternative Uses for Soils" (prepared for Bonn Conference, 1979).

There are many reasons for a developing country government to become involved in, or support, national agricultural research. The most general, aside from making sure that research takes place at all, would probably be to obtain the means (in terms of research output) to pursue its development objectives in agriculture and, more particularly, in food production. In addition to making the necessary resources available for investment and operation, this means that the government has to see to it that research focuses on the "right" crops, for example, those which enable the food needs of the majority of the population to be satisfied and which provide income (monetary or in kind) to those particularly in need. It has been argued that, in the past, certain crops were neglected in agricultural research because they were undervalued by the national price policy (44). Government support may help to compensate for this undervaluation. The other issue is to orient the research in such a way that small farmers can actually benefit from its results, given their cultivation practices and resource constraints (45).

The orientation of research towards a specific target group, such as resource-poor farmers, is seen by many as an important step away from past practice which deserves high priority (46). It implies special attention to the problems of women, and a decentralisation of the research effort to give due consideration to location-specific problems. As a consequence, however, the problem of research co-ordination within a country will gain in importance and special organisational efforts have to be made to provide a solution.

But even if we assume that research focusses on the "right" crop(s) and the "right" production environment, other tests to be passed are the effective adoption of the research results by farmers and the availability of adequate food supplies to those in need. The transmission of the research results, input supplies, remunerative prices and effective demand are necessary conditions to achieve these ends. As for effective demand, agricultural research holds the promise of reducing food production costs and prices (in real terms) over the longer run, so that even in a situation of stagnating per capita income, increasing satisfaction of food needs should be possible. All these essential conditions have been dealt with in varying degrees in this report. We shall limit ourselves here to elaborating further on extension services which, together with price policies, are a major area of government involvement in most developing countries.

b) Extension services: central element in the production support system

The relation between extension services and research has to be circular, i.e. research has to provide improved technology to extension services which, in the first place, should have provided guidance to research about a given problem area and, in a second stage, should feed back results and new problems to research.

It is erroneous to regard knowledge, physical inputs and material infrastructure as sufficient and straightforward ingredients for enhanced production. This assumes that technologies are "neutral" and produce certain results irrespective of the socio-political environment in which they are applied. In addition to the crucial matters of economic incentives and profitability, the final impact will depend on questions of organisation (who participates and how?) and the nature of the goods and services. These aspects have often tended to be neglected. In a study of Eastern India, T.K. Pal concludes that: "Farmers' requirements for improved rice varieties have not received adequate recognition in the breeding objectives of the rice breeders. The extension system has not acted as an effective intermediary between farmers and research workers" (47).

Government involvement in the production support system has both historical roots in the colonial past (48) and contemporary justifications. This is most evident for regulatory activities (quality and disease control, for example) and for the educational and infrastructural elements, but much less so for the provision of goods and services. The need for co-ordination and feedback among certain elements and social preoccupations (e.g. coverage of specific social groups and regions) are additional reasons for government involvement.

Distrust of private enterprise or simply the lack of private initiative have at times led governments to get involved in the supply of goods and services, but in practice they have rarely fulfilled this function completely. Governments have sometimes committed themselves to tasks beyond their capacity, thereby weakening the system as a whole by creating bottlenecks and making sub-optimal use of available resources (49). Commercial firms are not the only alternative to government involvement. Universities, churches and farmers' co-operatives are other possible actors in extension and input supply.

While often containing similar elements and facing similar problems, production support systems are specific to their socio-economic environment. They also vary with different crops and over time. Thus, there is no universally valid blueprint for such a system. But it may be useful to warn against certain pitfalls and to draw together positive elements which should help to design better policies in the future.

A Review of Shortcomings

The aim of this review is not to distribute blame, but to learn from past failures. These have been caused by misconceived ideas about the people involved and the appropriate extension message, as well as by problems of organisation, lack of resources and misguided investment decisions (50).

It is now generally recognised that a widespread error in extension education has been to assume that "farmers" and "male heads of household" are identical and consequently to make them the target of all extension education. In fact, women are doing much of the cultivation, in particular of food crops, but they are also heavily engaged in other crops. They must therefore be involved in extension and be provided with incentives to do the work required. Moreover, where changes have been introduced in areas not directly concerning women, consideration of how the consequences will affect them has often been forgotten. For example, the introduction of mechanisation generally allows an increase in the area cultivated, but the non-mechanised tasks carried out mostly by women increase proportionately, so that modernisation of this kind puts too heavy a burden on them. Similarly, where cash crops have been promoted in African countries, this has often meant additional work for women without a corresponding increase in their income. Although they draw on the help of women, men are responsible for cash crops and keep most of the cash income for themselves. Women then find it difficult to look after their food crops properly, and this has a negative impact on the availability of food at the household level, since cash income tends to be spent on non-food items.

Another common error has been to assume that if an input package is successfully adopted by some "progressive" farmers it will spread to all rural producers in due course. This assumption neglects existing social gaps between farmers, as well as differences in resource endowment and risk acceptance. Not only have these differences prevented poorer farmers from "copying" the bigger "progressive" farmers (51), but the unequal distribution of extension knowledge and material inputs has exacerbated income differentials and facilitated, in certain cases, the marginalisation of smaller farmers who, in periods of crop failure, have had to sell land or run into heavy debts.

Geographically concentrated area approaches and "pilot projects" have often been "technically successful" in increasing yields by introducing modern agricultural practices and inputs, accompanied by investments in infrastructure and social services (52). However, their cost per farmer has been much too high to allow widespread replication elsewhere. Similarly, production support activities have often been successful when they were concentrated on a specific crop. These were usually non-food crops or export crops (53), and staple crops were neglected.

Discrimination has not always been between food and non-food crops or between crops for the domestic market and export crops, but also between traditional and "modern" crops. Thus, rice and wheat received more support in Senegal than millet, although the latter is better adapted to the uncertain rainfall and shows lower losses of yield in years of drought (54). Such a strategy may, however, be justified if the differences in yield are very much in favour of rice and wheat and if sufficient provisions are made for years of drought.

Even where there has not been active discrimination against food crop production, it has often suffered from an inappropriate production support system, with regard to both the content of the extension message and the organisation of services. The advice offered, and the inputs suggested, to increase food production were frequently inappropriate to the specific ecological conditions of certain areas and to the resource constraints of small farmers. This may reflect inadequate research or poor links between researchers and extension agents. It has therefore been suggested, in the case of Northeast Thailand (55), for example, that extension workers should be assigned to crop experiment stations.

Modern extension teaching has sometimes scorned traditional cultivation practices (e.g. mulching and interplanting) and long established funds of information like the old Polynesian planting calendars are in danger of being lost. It tends to recommend the use of inputs which small farmers cannot always afford to buy because they are short of cash and unable or unwilling to take loans which represent too high a risk for them. Sometimes the inputs are simply not available at the time they are needed (56) or the extension message is not really a profitable proposition. Where institutional credit is available, small farmers find it difficult to obtain, either because they cannot provide the necessary collateral or because credit institutions shy away from the burden of small loans. Because of the formalities and delays involved, many small farmers are discouraged from undertaking the suggested intensification of production, or do so with much more expensive but uncomplicated loans from traditional money lenders. They may thus run into overly heavy debts which take away most, if not all, of the gains and may finally give up following the extension advice to use modern inputs.

As to the organisation of the various components of the production support system, there have been serious shortcomings in the past which are not necessarily specific to food production but which have nevertheless prevented food production from making full use of the existing resources. Thus, the lack of reliable farm management data for different types of farms hampers sensible planning at all levels. Parallel organisations for different crops sometimes make conflicting demands on farmers because they function in an unco-ordinated way. Where foreign "transplants" have been used to organise and operate extension systems, the longer-term need for indigenisation has not been recognised. The organisations were often of doubtful profitability for farmers and for the countries concerned in a longer perspective (57). Another problem area is the instability of organisation; frequent reorganisation and moving of senior staff tend to confuse farmers and to shake their confidence which is crucial to successful extension operations. Under the circumstances, farmers often become reluctant to follow extension advice and to introduce any innovations (58). Where extension staff is performing poorly, this is more often a problem of organisation, i.e. motivation, supervision and work planning, than one of lack of skill and training (59).

Finally, it should be mentioned that, with the exception of resource-intensive pilot projects, extension organisations are notoriously short of funds for operation. Thus, even when their structure, staffing and extension message are adequate, they may be inefficient due to a shortage of funds for transport or for very specific items which are essential parts of the extension package.

K.R.M. Anthony et al. warn against the danger of overloading the extension system ("over-extension") with functions which would better be carried out by others, for example, supply of fertilizer and debt collection. Extension education has to be seen as the genuine function; the supply of inputs and collection of produce may better be left to private purveyors or other agencies. "Extension systems are weakened when they perform roles other than those that contribute directly to agricultural production" (60).

Elements for Future Policies

Having reviewed the major shortcomings which prevent extension systems from promoting better use of resources for food production, one has to ask how they can be overcome or at least mitigated. Since the production support system is part of a wider food system, it should not be expected to solve all problems, particularly those lying beyond its own boundaries, such as price policy and marketing. The elements suggested here are necessary but not sufficient conditions to enhance food production.

a) Increased awareness of food problems

It seems that many of the weaknesses of production support systems stem from a lack of awareness of policy-makers of the precise nature of the food system and its problems. Such awareness has to be increased in each specific case, underlining the particular role of food production within the agricultural system and stressing the socio-economic and ecological diversity found within most countries. The food problem must not be seen only in terms of volumes of production, consumption, imports and exports but in terms of heterogeneous groups of producers and consumers.

b) Stronger linking of components

The various components of the production support system, i.e. extension services, input supply and infrastructure, not only have to be linked to each other (in their design and implementation, if not necessarily in terms of organisation) but must also be linked very closely to research and to the output delivery system. Feedback and flexibility should characterise these linkages, together with (at least) a clearing function for the government. As a rule, the Government will have some direct involvement in regulatory and educational functions and in the build-up of infrastructure.

c) Widespread impact

All components will have to be designed to assure that they reach the majority of producers (perhaps in different ways) instead of aiming only at a few and relying on imitation by others and a "trickling down" of benefits. This assumes that new methods have been thoroughly tested under the socio-economic and natural conditions in which they are to be introduced. Otherwise, blanket coverage can lead to important mistakes. Less proven innovations should be introduced only in a very selective way, so that any problems can be discovered and overcome before the mistakes are multiplied.

d) Target specificity

Widespread impact can only be achieved if measures are designed in a way which takes the particular situation of various groups of producers into account. This requires detailed knowledge about the socio-economic constraints and ecological conditions under which they operate. The poorest will deserve special attention since they usually find it more difficult to obtain access to services and inputs and might otherwise be further marginalised. Crop insurance may be one of the specific measures to be developed for the poorest farmers to enable them to cover the risks of innovation (61).

e) Profitability

Extension messages and input supplies will only be accepted and used by producers if they are clearly profitable for them and are perceived as such. Profitability for the country as a whole (in social cost-benefit terms) or for the government is not sufficient. Profitability has to be assured for the wide variety of conditions under which the target population operates. Small-scale activities, for example in irrigation, are often more profitable and more widely accessible than large-scale activities. The provision of a "minimum productive base" (62) may be necessary to assure profitability. In a similar vein, increased support for small stock, such as pigs, poultry, goats and sheep may be suggested. Mixed cropping is another promising avenue to enhance the profitability of small farm operations (63).

f) Organisational strength and flexibility

A production support system aiming at increased food production can be organised in many different ways but it needs a strong resource base, both financially and in terms of qualified, motivated and well-organised staff. To offer profitable innovations to large numbers of producers in different environments and socio-economic conditions requires a great deal of staff mobility and operational flexibility. To gain the confidence of producers and contribute to a self-sustaining development pattern, extension staff will have to be increasingly integrated into its area of operation, both socially and economically, i.e. it should draw increasingly on local resources and thus offer scope for effective participation (64) by the producers.

3. RECONSIDERING PRIORITIES AND POLICY OPTIONS

In the preceding chapters, some conclusions have been drawn about the ways in which priorities might be reconsidered by governments so as to meet the food needs of the population more adequately while also paying due attention to the various socio-economic constraints with which countries are faced. Very briefly, these conclusions suggest:

-- Identifying and implementing possibilities of reconciling the production of food crops for domestic consumption with the production of export crops, for example by making them mutually supportive or at least compatible in terms of resource requirements;

-- Establishing a balance between food import requirements and import capacity, for example by applying a selective policy of import substitution and production promotion, paying due attention to both the comparative advantage of the country and the implications for different categories of producers and consumers;

-- Reducing urban bias in the development strategy and in the allocation of resources;

-- Basing policies affecting the food system on analyses which distinguish between different groups of producers and consumers according to their resource endowment, needs, location and sociological patterns of behaviour.

There seems to be broad agreement in the literature and in policy statements of all kinds that food production for domestic consumption in the poorer countries, in particular by and for the most vulnerable groups of the population, deserves high priority. The underlying strategy has been referred to as "more of what we already know" but it is nevertheless "a sharp break from the practices of the past, a change of heart as regards food and agriculture, since a great deal of what we already know is not applied nearly widely enough, if at all" (65).

The World Food Council has acknowledged that a more self-reliant approach by countries is the starting point to overcome food problems (66). But "while recognising that many developing countries now [seek] to give a higher priority to food production, there [is] a large gap between declared policy and the means for its effective realisation" (67). The frequent ambiguity of policy statements can be illustrated with a quotation from President Nyerere of Tanzania: "Although we emphasize cash crops in our agricultural policy, our first aim is to provide sufficient and better food for everyone" (68).

In order to increase the institutional capacity for promoting food sector strategies, it has been suggested that developing countries create a "high-level co-ordinating authority" which would:

-- effectively raise the priority for food and harmonize policies related to food production and distribution and the improvement of nutrition in the country;

-- monitor and facilitate the formulation of a food and nutrition strategy and its food production, food distribution and nutrition-oriented programmes and projects; co-ordinate requests for specific external technical assistance for its formulation;

-- harmonize the country's efforts better to co-ordinate and monitor requests for external financial assistance for these projects; and

-- provide valuable backing to the responsible national departments or ministries in advancing claims for internal resources on behalf of important food sector needs (69).

The creation of such an institutional capacity does not prejudice the exact content of the food strategy of any given country. To the extent that most poor countries face an unfavourable world environment in the 1980s (i.e. limited export possibilities, high foreign exchange cost of urbanisation, including energy costs, poor prospects for increasing food aid, indebtedness, etc.), Lipton (70) suggests a temporary adjustment of the development pattern towards rural and urban subsistence modes of production. In his view, this adjustment should be brought about not by an all-out discrimination in favour of subsistence units but by arresting the present costly and risky "lean" against them. This kind of policy option links up with what has been said earlier about rural-urban relationships and will often pose difficult choices because it runs counter to existing power relationships and privileges.

To reduce food dependence and make better use of domestic resources, other authors suggest relying more on, and building upon, the traditional knowledge of farmers and adapting food consumption to domestic production possibilities. But they underline the need for diversification, e.g. into fruits (71).

Arguing mainly from an ecological point of view, but complementary to the suggestions of other authors and to the analysis presented in this report, Dahlberg (72) suggests greater emphasis on the conservation of basic resources (water, energy, soil, and plant varieties) than has been the case in conventional approaches to agricultural development. He also concludes that the well-being and development of the rural masses should receive priority over quantitative output targets and full integration of the peasants into complex agro-food systems.

Another area where governments may have to reconsider their options is the degree and nature of their involvement in the food system. While few would question the government's role in general incentive and support policies for the food system, there is considerable difference of opinion when it comes to day-to-day operations such as those implied in the marketing system (73). One school of thought, which seems to prevail in Latin America, sees consumers and producers threatened by monopolistic middlemen and suggests increased government intervention in the actual buying and selling of commodities, thus taking on the function of intermediaries (74). Others call for effective co-ordination between the private and public sectors in agricultural marketing. Finally, there are those who, based on experience of inefficient government interventions, suggest a minimum role for government. In a literature review of grain marketing systems in West Africa, Harriss analyses how the domestic marketing system may contribute to rural inequality and depress grain production, and how government intervention exacerbates this process (75). But the same author concludes that research findings are confusing and that "attempts to synthesise by unifying consensus seem to be guilty of over-simplification" (76). She also sees an ideological bias in recommendations which are anti-interventionist and pro-infrastructural.

Berg examines the options of the Sahel countries, many with de jure state monopolies in grain trade, in organising their marketing systems. These options are (a) to improve the status quo, (b) to introduce government monopolies where they do not exist and make them more effective and, (c) to move towards liberalisation and "light intervention". The last option is recommended because "it places fewest demands on formally trained manpower ... and avoids most of the contradictions inherent in government attempts to 'dominate' the grain market" (77). The main argument is that a decentralised private trading system tends to be more efficient than public trading agencies because the private system uses more appropriate technology, trading skills at low opportunity cost and relatively cheap transport services. But the option of "light intervention" leaves important functions of support (e.g. information, extension, training), supervision and crisis management to the government, which should protect producers and consumers against monopolistic abuses by traders.

The actual mix of public and private sector involvement in the marketing system will vary from one country to another, but will have to be based on considerations of both efficiency and equity corresponding to the aspirations and capacities of the government and the producers. Otherwise leakages, lack of response and illegal transactions will continue to counteract government policies and make them ineffective.

The scope for changing priorities and putting increased emphasis on food production, consumption and distribution is constrained by the availability of foreign exchange, investment funds and vested interests. It can be enlarged by foreign assistance in general (78) and by aid to agriculture in particular. The conditions under which food aid can not only avoid negative effects but provide support for agricultural development of the recipient country have been described in Chapter III of this report.

With regard to aid for agriculture, its potential contribution to the adjustment process lies not only in the level of resource transfer but also in its orientation. "The international community clearly must in no circumstances seek to take the place of the governments concerned, but it can help to identify and resolve problems, make suggestions, and, above all, maintain a dialogue" (79). More specifically, Johnson (80) suggests that high-income countries should support both location-specific and basic agricultural research, provide economic assistance to expand investment in agricultural production and rural infrastructure, and reduce trade barriers so as to increase the economic opportunities of developing countries.

The evolution of official commitments to food and agriculture by all donor groups (other than communist countries) is shown in Table 20, indicating that commitments have increased in real value by 149 per cent between 1973 and 1981. Commitments to this sector have grown faster than total aid commitments, reaching 28.9 per cent of total commitments in 1978. There was a levelling off in the increase of aid to this sector in 1979 and 1980, but commitments picked up again considerably in 1981. Aid to food and agriculture continues to have priority in most DAC bilateral aid programmes. The 1980

Table 20

OFFICIAL COMMITMENTS TO FOOD AND AGRICULTURE AT CURRENT PRICES
AND CONSTANT PRICES, 1973-1981

($ million)

COMMITMENTS BY SOURCE AND TYPE	AT CURRENT PRICES									AT CONSTANT PRICES (1979)								
	1973	1974	1975	1976	1977	1978	1979	1980	1981	1973	1974	1975	1976	1977	1978	1979	1980	1981
DAC MEMBERS' BILATERAL ODA	810	1 700	1 644	1 624	2 597	3 270	4 304	4 228	4 261	1 594	2 819	2 359	2 246	3 279	3 633	4 304	3 809	3 839
MULTILATERAL ODA	725	1 001	1 056	1 257	1 621	2 402	2 503	3 266	3 299	1 533	1 833	1 530	1 814	2 139	2 761	2 503	2 969	3 083
OPEC ODA	34	133	446	273	365	276	243	199	374	69	218	640	378	461	307	243	179	346
TOTAL ODA	1 569	2 834	3 145	3 154	4 583	5 948	7 050	7 693	7 934	3 196	4 870	4 529	4 438	5 879	6 701	7 050	6 957	7 268
Percentage change	n.a.	+81	+11	--	+45	+30	+20	+9	+3	n.a.	+52	-6	-2	+32	+14	+5	--1	+4
DAC MEMBERS OOF	172	168	86	268	120	353	329	265	569	351	275	137	395	159	403	329	237	527
MULTILATERAL OOF	442	982	1 846	1 458	2 123	2 872	2 319	2 935	3 646	902	1 610	2 944	2 150	2 816	3 275	2 319	2 621	3 376
OPEC OOF	31	55	209	150	60	42	99	54	81	63	90	333	221	80	49	99	48	75
TOTAL OOF	645	1 205	2 141	1 876	2 303	3 267	2 747	3 254	4 296	1 316	1 975	3 414	2 766	3 055	3 727	2 747	2 906	3 978
Percentage change	n.a.	+87	+78	-15	+24	+42	--16	+18	+32	n.a.	+50	+60	-19	+10	+22	-26	+6	+37
DAC MEMBERS' BILATERAL ODA + OOF	982	1 868	1 730	1 892	2 717	3 617	4 633	4 493	4 830	1 945	3 094	2 496	2 641	4 338	4 036	4 633	4 040	4 366
MULTILATERAL ODA + OOF	1 167	1 983	2 902	2 715	3 744	5 274	4 822	6 201	6 945	2 435	3 443	4 474	3 964	4 955	6 036	4 822	5 590	6 459
OPEC ODA + OOF	65	188	655	423	425	320	342	253	455	132	308	973	599	541	346	342	227	421
GRAND TOTAL OFFICIAL COMMITMENTS (ODA + OOF)	2 214	4 039	5 286	5 030	6 886	9 211	9 797	10 947	12 230	4 512	6 845	7 943	7 204	8 934	10 428	9 797	9 863	11 246
Percentage change	n.a.	+82	+31	-5	+37	+34	+6	+11	+12	n.a.	+52	+16	-9	+24	+17	--6	+1	+14

Source: OECD

Abbreviations used:

DAC: Development Assistance Committee
ODA: Official Development Assistance
OPEC: Organisation for Petroleum Exporting Countries
OOF: Other Official Flows

n.a.: not available

129

decline can be largely attributed to accidental variations and delays in project preparation. Multilateral institutions continue to give particular
priority to aid to food and agriculture, allocating more than 40 per cent of
their total commitments to this sector in 1981.

From the statistics available globally, it is impossible to distinguish
clearly between aid to food and non-food agriculture (81). But from individual programmes, and from the general support given by DAC countries to
"food strategies" and the "food system" approach, it appears that growing
emphasis has been given to the food sector (82).

However, the level of foreign assistance to agriculture in general has
been insufficient in view of the objective set for the 1970s in the International Development Strategy for the second "Development Decade", i.e. 4 per
cent annual production increase (83). FAO and the World Food Council set the
annual requirements of aid to agriculture for the period 1975-1980 at
$8.3 billion in 1975 prices, but the recent shortfall amounted to about 40 per
cent of that level (84). FAO further estimates the requirements for 1990 at
$11-12.5 billion and for 2000 at some $15-18 billion at 1975 prices.

In order to make foreign assistance contribute effectively to a change
in priorities and policies in support of the food sector, it has to be allocated to those countries whose governments are willing to commit their prestige and resources to such a change and are ready to take the necessary steps
with respect to pricing, taxation, investment, etc. (85). Without such
measures, foreign assistance can have little impact.

NOTES AND REFERENCES

1. See The Global 2000 Report to the President, prepared by the Council on Environmental Quality and the Department of State, Washington, D.C., 1980, and, FAO, Agriculture: Towards 2000, Rome, 1981, henceforth referred to as "FAO, AT 2000".

2. See FAO, op. cit., Statistical Summary.

3. IFPRI (International Food Policy Research Institute), Food Needs of Developing Countries, Research Report No. 3, Washington, D.C., December 1977, p. 22.

4. FAO, op. cit., p. 22.

5. J. Lombard, "Une autre 'fin des paysans' : Ceux d'Afrique Noire", in Revue Tiers Monde, Vol. XXII, No. 85, 1981, pp. 40-41.

6. A. Sen, Poverty and Famine, An Essay on Entitlement and Deprivation, Clarendon Press, Oxford, 1981.

7. For a conceptual model of the causes of hunger, see U. Jonsson, "The Causes of Hunger", in Food and Nutrition Bulletin, Vol. 3, No. 2, United Nations University, April 1981, pp. 1-9.

8. P. Pinstrup-Andersen, "Policy Options for Short-Run Expansions of Food Consumption Among Food-Deficit Households in Sub-Saharan Africa", in IFPRI, Food Policy Issues and Concerns in Sub-Saharan Africa, Papers prepared for a meeting in Ibadan, Nigeria, 9-11 February 1981, p. 145.

9. See also E. Lefranc, "Social Structure, Land Use and Food Availability in the Caribbean", in Food and Nutrition Bulletin, Vol. 3, No. 4, United Nations University, October 1981.

10. See S.K. Kumar, "Nutrition Concerns on Food Policy for Sub-Saharan Africa", in IFPRI (1981), op. cit., pp. 81-102.

11. See also S.K. Kumar, ibid., p. 92.

12. For Korea's experience with such a scheme, see Dong-Hi Kim and Yong-Jae Joo, The Food Situation and Policies in the Republic of Korea, OECD Development Centre, Paris, 1982.

13. A.A. Saleh and O.H. Goolsby, "Institutional Disincentives to Agricultural Production in Developing Countries", in Foreign Agriculture, Supplement, August 1977, US Department of Agriculture, p. 1; this article provides a detailed overview of disincentive measures by country, type of disincentive and commodity.

14. FAO, "Towards 2000", C79/24, Rome, July 1979, p. 166.

15. For the case of Venezuela, see John Sweeney, "Agriculture Stagnates as Pledged Reforms Remain Unfulfilled", in International Herald Tribune, Special Supplement on Venezuela, May 1980, quoting President Herrera with this diagnosis.

16. Elliot Berg, "Marketing, Price Policy and Storage of Food Grains in the Sahel: A Diagnostic Survey", Executive Summary, p. 13, Paper submitted to the CILSS/Club du Sahel Colloquium in Nouakchott, 2-6 July, 1979.

17. John Mellor, "Agricultural Price Policy and Income Distribution in Low Income Countries", World Bank Working Paper No. 214, September 1975, p. 12. Mellor distinguishes the case of static technology from that of technological change.

18. See, for example, H. Dupriez, Paysans d'Afrique Noire, ed. Terres et Vie, Nivelles (Belgium), 1980, p. 154, on depressed cereal prices as compared to prices for cotton in Chad; similarly, Mamady Keith, "Le coton ne se mange pas", in l'Economiste du tiers monde, No. 31, January 1979, pp. 17-18.

19. See T.W. Schultz (ed.), Distortions of Agricultural Incentives, Indiana University Press, Bloomington, Indiana and London, 1978, pp. 14-17.

20. See Yukon Huang, "Backward-bending Supply Curves and Behaviour of Subsistence Farmers", in Journal of Development Studies, Vol. 12, No. 3, April 1976, pp. 191-211.

21. Willis L. Peterson, "International Farm Prices and the Social Cost of Cheap Food Policies", in American Journal of Agricultural Economics, Vol. 61, No. 1, February 1979, pp. 12-21; this conclusion is based on an analysis of evidence from 27 countries. See also G.T. Brown, "Agricultural Pricing Policies in Developing Countries", in T.W. Schultz, op. cit., p. 88, D.C. Faber et al., "Normative Study of the Supply Response of Rice in Thailand", DAE-CARD Sector Analysis Series, No. 13, Iowa State University, 1978.

22. R. Barker and Y. Hayami, "Price Support Versus Input Subsidy for Food Self-Sufficiency in Developing Countries", in American Journal of Agricultural Economics, Vol. 58, No. 4, 1976, pp. 617-628.

23. Raisuddin Ahmed, "Price Support Versus Fertilizer Subsidy for Increasing Rice Production in Bangladesh", in Bangladesh Development Studies, Vol. VI, No. 2, 1978, pp. 119-138.

24. See, for example, G.T. Brown, op. cit., pp. 92-93.

25. FAO (1979), op. cit., p. 167, lists Colombia, Costa Rica, Guyana and Mexico for a variety of crops and Brazil for wheat; Malaysia, the Republic of Korea, Kenya, Malawi, Zaire, Chad, Niger and Upper Volta for their major food crops.

26. See E. Berg, op. cit., p. 11 with regard to Sahel countries.

27. For stabilization through international trade see D. Bigman and S. Reutlinger, "National and International Policies Toward Food Security and Price Stabilization", in American Economic Review, May, 1979, pp. 159-163.

28. See, for example, Arthur J. Mann, "Agricultural Price Stabilization Policy in a Developing Economy: The Case of the Dominican Republic", in Social and Economic Studies, Vol. 26, No. 2, June 1977, pp. 190-201.

29. See, for example, J. Mellor, op. cit.

30. Ibid., p. 11.

31. See also FAO (1981), op. cit., pp. 87-88.

32. J. Mellor, op. cit., p. 8.

33. This course of action is suggested for Indonesia by C.P. Timmer and H. Alderman, "Estimating Consumption Parameters for Food Policy Analysis", in American Journal of Agricultural Economics, Vol. 61, No. 5, December 1979, Proceedings Issue, pp. 982-987.

34. It has been estimated that the sources of additional crop production up to the year 2000 will be area expansion for 26 per cent and yield increases and more intensive cropping for 74 per cent; see FAO (1981), op. cit., p.61. With regard to the African production potential, see P.A. Oram, "Production Potentials in Africa: Issues and Strategies", in IFPRI (1981), op. cit., pp. 45-80, and Higgins et al., "Africa's Agricultural Potential", in CERES, No. 83, September-October 1981, pp. 13-21.

35. Research needs were reviewed at a Conference held in Bonn, Germany in 1979, the proceedings of which are summarised in Rockefeller Foundation (ed.), Agricultural Production, Research and Development Strategies for the 1980s, New York, 1980. We shall draw here on some of the papers submitted to that Conference.

36. For a general description of the policy conditions providing a favourable environment for farmers, see D.G. Johnson, The Politics of Food, Chicago Council on Foreign Relations, Chicago, 1980, pp. 6-10.

37. See the Special Issues on Post-Harvest Food Losses of the Food and Nutrition Bulletin, Vol. 4, No. 2, April 1982, in particular the article by P.S. Tyler on "Misconception of Food Losses". See also National Academy of Sciences, Post-Harvest Food Losses in Developing Countries, Washington, D.C., 1978, which contains a very comprehensive treatment of the subject based on contributions from all parts of the world and includes a list of organisations actively involved in post-harvest food conservation.

38. G. Levine et al., "Draft State of Knowledge Report for the Water Resources Task Group" (Bonn Conference, 1979), p. 97.

39.   C.F. Bentley et al., "Enhancing Agricultural Production: Potentials, Constraints and Alternative Uses for Soils", (Bonn Conference, 1979), pp. 82-83.

40.   A similar emphasis is suggested by the World Development Report, 1980, World Bank, which states that "the key to greater food production lies in a breakthrough in dry land farming" (p. 23). With regard to Sahel countries, priority for rainfed agriculture is suggested by J. Lantier, "l'Eau et les hommes", in l'Economiste du Tiers Monde, No. 51, October 1980, pp. 24-25.

41.   John Mellor, "Africa: Depressing Trends and a Difficult Task", in IFPRI Report, Vol. 2, No. 2, May 1980.

42.   Peter Oram, "The Investment Tripod: Infrastructure, Technology and Training", in IFPRI Report, Vol. 2, No. 1, January 1980.

43.   For suggestions as to the relationships between national and international centres, see Robert E. Evenson, "The Organisation of Research to Improve Crops and Animals in Low-Income Countries", in T.W. Schultz, op. cit., pp. 233-245. A workshop on "Strengthening National Agriculture Research" was held by SAREC (Swedish Agency for Research Cooperation with Developing Countries) in September 1979, at which papers on national agricultural research in the following developing countries were presented: Africa: Botswana, Egypt, Ethiopia, Ghana, Guinea-Bissau, Kenya, Tanzania, Zambia; Asia: Bangladesh, India, Indonesia, Pakistan, Sri Lanka, Thailand; South and Central America: Brazil, Costa Rica, Guyana, Jamaica, Trinidad and Tobago.

44.   See, for example, R.E. Evenson, op. cit.; similarly T.W. Schultz, op. cit. A similar effect may have been achieved where low prices resulted from the market situation rather than from government policy.

45.   The development of local crops which can, of course, also satisfy other objectives, among which the desire for increased food self-sufficiency, has gained heightened attention in certain countries in recent years.

46.   See B. Bengtsson, "Strengthening National Agricultural Research", Report from a SAREC Workshop, Part II, Summary and Conclusions, Stockholm, 1980, pp. 18-19.

47.   T.K. Pal, "Productivity and Constraints in Rainfed Lowland Rice Farming in Eastern India", in IRRI, Rainfed Lowland Rice, Selected Papers from the 1978 International Rice Research Conference, Los Banos, 1979, p. 313.

48.   See K.R.M. Anthony et al., Agricultural Change in Tropical Africa, Cornell University Press, Ithaca, 1979, p. 224.

49.   K. Osafo-Gyimah finds a similar conclusion in his review of several authors' assessment of government food policy in the Nkrumah era; see K. Osafo-Gyimah, "Rural Development and Food Policies in Ghana", paper submitted to CODESRIA-CAFRAD Conference on Integrated Urban and Rural Development in Africa, Dakar, 2-4 June 1980.

50. See, also D. Benor and J.Q. Harrison, "Agricultural Extension, The Training and Visit System", World Bank, 1977, for a short review of general problems with extension and how they are tackled by the "training and visit" system.

51. See, for example, T.K. Pal, op. cit., p. 311, who suggests that "poverty is the most serious constraint to the use of modern rices".

52. Among the well-documented examples are the Lilongwe Programme in Malawi and CADU in Ethiopia.

53. K.R.M. Anthony et al., op. cit., p. 242.

54. See Bernard Founou-Tchuigoua, "Stratégie de l'autosuffisance alimentaire et choix d'une céréale prioritaire au Sénégal", 1980, mimeo.

55. See K. Adulavidhaya, "Socio-Economic Aspects of Rice Production in Northeast Thailand", in IRRI, "Rainfed Lowland Rice", op. cit., p. 323.

56. See, for example, E. Ahsan, "Rainfed Lowland Rice Farming in Bangladesh -- Productivity and Constraints", in IRRI, op. cit., p. 304.

57. See K.R.M. Anthony et al., op. cit., pp. 230-231.

58. See, for example, the case of Ghana reported by K. Osafo-Gyimah, op. cit., p. 18.

59. See K.R.M. Anthony et al., op. cit., p. 233.

60. Ibid., pp. 245-246.

61. For the mechanisms of such a scheme applied to empirical data from Bangladesh, see R.W. Herdt, M.M. Dehn, "Insurance for Small Farmers to Encourage Innovation", in Bangladesh Development Studies, Vol. 6, No. 2, 1978, pp. 191-200.

62. See K. Griffin, "Growth and Impoverishment in the Rural Areas of Asia", in World Development, Vol. 7, 1979, p. 379.

63. The East-West Resource Systems Institute's research indicates that "land use efficiency can be increased by 20 to 50 per cent by combining a cereal crop like maize with legume crops like soybean, cowpea and mungbean, rather than by growing them separately.", EWRSI Newsletter, Vol. 2, No. 1, 1980, p. 8.

64. It has been suggested to involve farmers in both the planning and implementation stage to give greater emphasis to the existing farming system; see J. Dey, "Development Planning in the Gambia: The Gap Between Planners' and Farmers' Perceptions, Expectations and Objectives", in World Development, Vol. 10, No. 5, 1982, pp. 377-396.

65. FAO (1981), op. cit., p. 125; the more concrete implications of that development strategy for food and agriculture are elaborated upon on pp. 126-130.

66. See World Food Council, "Toward a World Without Hunger: Progress and Prospects for Completing the Unfinished Agenda of the World Food Conference", Report by the Executive Director, WFC/1979/3, p. 36.

67. World Food Council, "Conclusions of the Consolidating Meeting on Improved Food Production, Nutrition and Investment in Developing Countries", Bellagio, 2-6 April, 1979, p. 1.

68. Quoted by U. Jonsson, "Towards a Food and Nutrition Policy in Tanzania", in Food Policy, May, 1980, pp. 143-147.

69. World Food Council, "Conclusions of the Consolidating Meeting on Improved Food Production, Nutrition and Investment in Developing Countries", op. cit., pp. 4-5.

70. See M. Lipton "Rural Development and the Retention of the Rural Populations in the Countryside of Developing Countries", paper delivered at the 12th IIDC Conference in Ottawa, October 1981 (revised version published in the Canadian Journal of Development Studies, Vol. 3, No. 1, 1982).

71. See P. Spitz, "Systèmes alimentaires et indépendance nationale", and C. Chaulet, "Eloge du couscous", both papers submitted to a seminar on the Evolution of Algerian Food Consumption, Centre de Recherche en Economie Appliquée, Algiers, June 1981.

72. K.A. Dahlberg, Beyond the Green Revolution, The Ecology and Politics of Global Agricultural Development, Plenum Press, New York, 1979, p. 212.

73. See also OECD/FAO, Critical Issues in Food Marketing Systems in Developing Countries, Report of the OECD/FAO Joint Seminar, Paris, 18-22 October, 1976.

74. See K. Harrison, "Public Policies and the Development of Agricultural Marketing Systems", in Proceedings of the Seminar on Agricultural Policy: A Limiting Factor in the Development Process, 17-21 March, 1975, Inter-American Development Bank, Washington, D.C., p. 355; as an example see S. Almeida et al., "Analysis of Traditional Strategies to Combat World Hunger and Their Results", in International Journal of Health Services, Vol. 5, No. 1, 1975, pp. 121-141.

75. B. Harriss, "Going Against the Grain", in Development and Change, Vol. 10, No. 3, July 1979, pp. 363-384; for negative experiences in India and Peru, see G.T. Brown, op. cit., pp. 91-92.

76. B. Harriss, "There is Method in My Madness: Or is it Vice Versa? Measuring Agricultural Market Performance", in Food Research Institute Studies, Vol. XVII, No. 2, 1979.

77. E. Berg, op. cit., p. 9.

78. For estimates of the effect of different assistance levels on African economies, see The World Bank, Accelerated Development in Sub-Saharan Africa, Washington, D.C., 1980, pp. 122-124.

DE CASTRO, L.R.,
    "Brazil's Farm Conflict", in South, July 1981.

DEATON, B.J.,
    "Public Law 480 -- The Critical Choices", in American Journal of Agri-
    cultural Economics, Vol. 62, N° 5, December 1980.

DELORME, H.,
    "L'Algérie: importations de céréales. Blocage de la Production et
    Développement de l'Etat", in Maghreb Machrek, N° 91, 1981.

DEPARTEMENT DU PLAN,
    "Programme de relance agricole 1978-1980", Kinshasa, 1978.

DEY, J.,
    "Development Planning in the Gambia: The Gap Between Planners and
    Farmers' Perceptions. Expectations and Objectives", in World Develop-
    ment, Vol. 10, N° 5, 1982.

DUPRIEZ, H.,
    Paysans d'Afrique Noire, Ed. Terres et Vie, Nivelles (Belgium), 1980.

ECKHOLM, E.P.,
    Losing Ground: Environmental Stress and World Food Prospects, World-
    watch Institute, Washington, D.C., 1976.

ECKSTEIN, S., et al.,
    "Land Reform in Latin America: Bolivia, Chile, Mexico, Peru and
    Venezuela", World Bank Staff Working Paper N° 275, Washington,
    D.C., 1978.

FABER, D.C., et al.,
    "Normative Study of the Supply Response of Rice in Thailand", DAE-Card
    Sector Analysis Series N° 13, Iowa State University, 1978.

FAO,   "Agriculture: Towards 2000", C79/24, July 1979.

FAO,   Agriculture: Towards 2000, Rome, 1981.

FAO,   Production Yearbook, various editions.

FAO,   Fertilizer Yearbook, various editions.

FAO,   Trade Yearbook, various editions.

FAO,   "Examen et analyse de la réforme agraire et du développement rural dans
       les pays en voie de développement depuis le milieu des années
       soixante", CMRADR/INF.3, Rome, 1979.

FAO,   Annual Fertilizer Review, 1972.

FAO,   "Monthly Bulletin of Statistics", Vol. 4, March 1981.

FAO,   "Food Aid Bulletin", N° 4, Rome, 1980.

FAO,   The Fourth World Food Survey, Rome, 1977.

FAO,   "Conférence mondiale sur la réforme agraire et le développement rural", Rome, 12-20 July, 1979, Report (WCARRD/REP).

FARMER, B.H., (ed.),
        Green Revolution?, MacMillan, London, 1977.

FEDERAL MINISTRY OF AGRICULTURE,
        "Agricultural Development in Nigeria: 1973-1985", Lagos, 1974.

FOUNOU-TCHUIGOUA, B.,
        "Stratégie de l'autosuffisance alimentaire et choix d'une céréale prioritaire au Sénégal", 1980, mimeo.

GASSOU, A.,
        "Un Togo prospère, fier et autosuffisant", in Afrique Agriculture, N° 72, August 1981.

GAVAN, J.D.,
        CHANDRASEKERA, I.S., "The Impact of Public Foodgrain Distribution on Food Consumption and Welfare in Sri Lanka", IFPRI Research Report N° 13, Washington, D.C., December 1978.

GEORGE, S.,
        Les Stratèges de la faim, Editions Grounauer, Geneva, 1981.

GHERSI, G., et al.,
        Multinational Firms and Agro-Food Systems in Developing Countries: A Bibliographic Review, OECD Development Centre, 1981.

GIRDNER, J., et al.,
        "Ghana's Agricultural Food Policy -- Operation Feed Yourself", in Food Policy, Vol. 5, N° 1, 1980.

GOLDBERG, R.,
        "The Role of the Multinational Corporation", in American Journal of Agricultural Economics, Vol. 63, N° 2, May 1981.

GOUELI, A.A.,
        "Food Security Programme in Egypt", in VALDES, A. (ed.), Food Security for Developing Countries, Westview Press, Boulder, 1981.

GREEN, M.B.,
        Eating Oil, Energy Use in Food Production, Westview Press, Boulder, 1978.

GRIFFIN, K., JAMES, J.,
        The Transition to Egalitarian Development, Economic Policies for Structural Change in the Third World, MacMillan Press, London, 1981.

GRIFFIN, K.,
        "Growth and Impoverishment in the Rural Areas of Asia", in World Development, Vol. 7, 1979.

HANSON, H.,
"Plant and Animal Resources for Food Production by Developing Countries in the 1980's", Paper prepared for Conference on Agricultural Production, Bonn, 8-12 October 1979.

HARRIS, G.T.,
"Replacing Imported Food Supplies to Port Moresby (Papua New Guinea)", Occasional Paper N° 17, Development Studies Centre, Australian National University, Canberra, 1980.

HARRISON, K.,
"Public Policies and the Development of the Agricultural Marketing Systems", in Proceedings of the Seminar on Agricultural Policy: A Limiting Factor in the Development Process, Inter-American Development Bank, Washington, D.C., 17-21 March 1975.

HARRISS, B.,
"Going Against the Grain", in Development and Change, Vol. 10, N° 3, July 1979.

HARRISS, B.,
"There is Method In My Madness: Or Is It Vice Versa?: Measuring Agricultural Market Performance", in Food Research Institute Studies, Vol. 17, N° 2, 1979.

HERDT, R.W., DEHN, M.M.,
"Insurance for Small Farmers to Encourage Innovation", in Bangladesh Development Studies, Vol. 6, N° 2, 1978.

HIGGINS, A., et al.,
"Africa's Agricultural Potential", in Cérès, N° 83, September-October 1981.

HILLMAN, J.S.,
"The Role of Export Cropping in Less Developed Countries", in American Journal of Agricultural Economics, Vol. 63, N° 2, May 1981.

HUANG, Y.,
"Backward-Bending Supply Curves and Behavior of Subsistence Farmers", in Journal of Development Studies, Vol. 12, N° 3, April 1976.

HUDDLESTON, B.,
"Responsiveness of Food Aid to Variable Import Requirements", in VALDES, A. (Ed.), Food Security for Developing Countries, Westview Press, Boulder, 1981.

IFPRI, "Food Needs of Developing Countries", Research Report N° 3, Washington, D.C., December 1977.

JANVRY, A. de, GROUND, L.,
"Types and Consequences of Land Reform in Latin America", in Latin American Perspectives, 19(1979): 96.

JEQUIER, N.,
      Appropriate Technology: Problems and Promises, OECD Development
      Centre, Paris, 1976.

JOHNSON, D.G.,
      The Politics of Food, Chicago Council on Foreign Relations,
      Chicago, 1980.

JONSSON, U.,
      "Towards a Food and Nutrition Policy in Tanzania", in Food Policy,
      May 1980.

JONSSON, U.,
      "The Causes of Hunger", in Food and Nutrition Bulletin, Vol. 3, N° 2,
      United Nations University, April 1981.

JOSLING, T.,
      "International Trade and World Food Production", in JOHNSON, D.G.
      (ed.), The Politics of Food, The Chicago Council on Foreign Relations,
      Chicago, 1980.

KILEY-WORTHINGTON, M.,
      "Problems of Modern Agriculture", in Food Policy, Vol. 5, N° 3, 1980.

KLATZMAN, J.,
      "Besoins alimentaires et potentialités des pays en voie de développe-
      ment", in Mondes en Développement, N° 29-30, 1980.

KUMAR, S.R.,
      "Nutrition Concerns in Food Policy for Sub-Saharan Africa", in IFPRI,
      Food Policy Issues and Concerns in Sub-Saharan Africa, Washington,
      D.C., 1981.

LABONNE, M., HIBON, A.,
      "Futur agricole et alimentaire de la méditerranée arabe", INRA,
      December 1978.

LAMPE, K., et al.,
      "Agricultural Production: Research and Development Stategies for the
      1980s. Conclusions and Recommendations of the Bonn Conférence 8-12
      October 1979", Rockefeller Foundation, 1980.

LANE, S.,
      "The Contribution of Food Aid to Nutrition", in American Journal of
      Agricultural Economics, Vol. 62, N° 5, December 1980.

LANTIER, J.,
      "L'Eau et les hommes", in l'Economiste du Tiers Monde, N° 51,
      October 1980.

LAPPE, F.M., COLLINS, J.,
      Food First: Beyond the Myth of Scarcity, Houghton Mifflin,
      Boston, 1977.

LAPPE, M., et al.,
"Aid as Obstacle", Institute for Food and Development Policy, San Francisco, 1981.

LEFRANC, E.,
"Social Structure. Land Use and Food Availability in the Caribbean", in Food and Nutrition Bulletin, Vol. 3, N° 4, United Nations University, October 1981.

LEHMANN, D.,
"Political Framework for Nutrition Policies", in Food and Nutrition Bulletin, Vol. 1, N° 1, United Nations University, October 1978.

LELE, U., CANDLER, W.,
"Food Security: Some East African Considerations", in VALDES, A. (Ed.), Food Security for Developing Countries, Westview Press, Boulder, 1981.

LEVINE, G., et al.,
"Draft State of Knowledge Report for the Water Resources Task Group", Bonn Conference, 1979.

LEWIS, J.P., 1981 Review of Development Co-operation, OECD, 1981.

LIPTON, M.,
Why Poor People Stay Poor - A Study of Urban Bias in World Development, Temple Smith, London, 1977.

LIPTON, M.,
"Technological Cures for Social Pathologies", in The Journal of Development Studies, Vol. 15, N° 4, July 1979.

LIVINGSTON, I., ORD, H.W.,
Agricultural Economics for Tropical Africa, Heinemann, London, 1981.

LOMBARD, J.,
"Une autre 'fin des paysans' : ceux d'Afrique noire", in Revue Tiers Monde, Vol. 22, N° 85, 1981.

MAMADY, K.,
"Le coton ne se mange pas", in l'Economiste du Tiers Monde, N° 31, January 1979.

MANN, A.J.,
"Agricultural Price Stabilization Policy in a Developing Economy: The Case of the Dominican Republic", in Social and Economic Studies, Vol. 26, N° 2, June 1977.

MAYER, J., DWYER, J.T.,
Food and Nutrition Policy in a Changing World, Oxford University Press, New York, 1979.

MCINERNEY, J.P., DONALDSON, G.J.,
"The Consequences of Farm Tractors in Pakistan", World Bank Staff Working Paper N° 210, Washington, D.C., 1975

MELLOR, J.W.,
"Agricultural Price Policy and Income Distribution in Low-Income Countries", World Bank Paper N° 214, Washington, D.C., September 1975.

MELLOR, J.,
"Africa: Depressing Trends and a Difficult Task", in IFPRI Report,
Vol. 2, N° 2, May 1980.

MELLOR, J.W.,
"Food Aid and Nutrition", in American Journal of Agricultural Economics, Vol. 62, N° 5, December 1980.

MORGAN, D.,
The Merchants of Grain, Viking Press, New York, 1979.

MURDOCH, W.W.,
The Poverty of Nations - The Political Economy of Hunger and Population, Johns Hopkins University Press, Baltimore, 1980.

NATIONAL ACADEMY OF SCIENCES,
Post-Harvest Food Losses in Developing Countries, Washington D.C., 1978.

NEWLAND, K.,
"City Limits: Emerging Constraints on Urban Growth", Worldwatch Paper
N° 38, Washington, D.C., 1980.

OECD/FAO,
"Critical Issues in Food Marketing Systems in Developing Countries",
Report of the OECD/FAO Joint Seminar, Paris, 18-22 October, 1976.

OESTERDIEKHOFF, P., WOHLMUT, K.,
"Handlungsspielraeume des Unterentwickelten Agrarlandes Sudan", in
Diskurs, University of Bremen, N° 3, August 1980.

OESTERDIEKHOFF, P.,
"Neue Weltwirtschaftsordnung und Kleinbaeuerliche Exportproduktion in
LLDC's, in Diskurs, N° 3, August 1980.

ORAM, P.,
"The Investment Tripod: Infrastructure, Technology and Training", in
IFPRI Report, Vol. 2, N° 1, January 1980.

OSAFO-GYIMAH, K.,
"Rural Development and Food Policies in Ghana", Paper submitted to
CODESRIA-CAFRAD Conference on Integrated Urban and Rural Development in
Africa, Dakar, 2-4 June 1980.

PAL, T.K.,
"Productivity and Constraints in Rainfed Lowland Rice Farming in
Eastern India", in IRRI. Rainfed Lowland Rice, Selected papers from
the 1978 International Rice Research Conference, Los Banos, 1979.

PARKINSON, J.,
"Food Aid", in FAALAND, J. (Ed.), Aid and Influence - The Case of Bangladesh, MacMillan, London, 1981.

PEARSE, A.,
Seeds of Plenty. Seeds of Want. Social and Economic Implications of the Green Revolution, Clarendon Press, Oxford, 1980.

PETERSON, W.L.,
"International Farm Prices and the Social Cost of Cheap Food Policies", in American Journal of Agricultural Economics, Vol. 61, N° 1, February 1979.

PINSTRUP-ANDERSON, P.,
"Policy Options for Short-Run Expansions of Food Consumption Among Food-Deficit Households in Sub-Saharan Africa", in IFPRI. Food Policy Issues and Concerns in Sub-Saharan Africa, Papers prepared for a meeting in Ibadan (Nigeria), 9-11 February 1981

PRIEBE, H., HANKEL, W.,
"Der Agrarsektor im Entwicklungsprozess", in Entwicklung und Zusammenarbeit, N° 5, 1981.

RAISUDDIN, A.,
"Price Support Versus Fertilizer Subsidy for Increasing Rice Production in Bangladesh", in Bangladesh Development Studies, Vol. 6, N° 2, 1978.

RAO, V., CHOTIGEAT, T.,
"The Inverse Relationship Between Size of Holdings and Agricultural Productivity", in American Journal of Agricultural Economics, August 1981.

REUTLINGER, S., SELOWSKY,
"Malnutrition and Poverty: Magnitude and Policy Options", World Bank Occasional Paper N° 23, 1976.

ROCKEFELLER FOUNDATION (Ed.),
Agricultural Production. Research and Development Strategies for the 1980s, New York, 1980.

SAI, F.T.,
"Food; Population and Politics", Occasional Essay N° 3, International Planned Parenthood Federation, London, 1977.

SALEH, A.A., GOOLSBY, O.H.,
"Institutional Disincentives to Agricultural Production in Developing Countries", in Foreign Agriculture, Supplement, U.S. Department of Agriculture, August 1977.

SAWADOGO, A.,
L'Agriculture en Côte d'Ivoire, Presses Universitaires de France, Paris, 1977.

SCHERTENLEIB, J.,
  "Schweizer Nahrungsmittelhilfe -- Begruendung, Wirkungen, Postulate",
  Entwicklungspolitische Diskussionsbeitraege N° 21, Institut füer
  Sozialethic des SEK Entwicklungsstudien, Adliswil, 1981.

SCHNEIDER, H.,
  Food Aid for Development, OECD Development Centre, Paris, 1978.

SCHULTZ, T.W., (ed.),
  Distortions of Agricultural Incentives, Indiana University Press,
  Bloomington, Indiana and London, 1978.

SELOWSKY, M.,
  "Target Group-Oriented Food Programmes: Cost-Effectiveness Com-
  parisons", in American Journal of Agricultural Economics, Vol. 61,
  N° 5, December 1979.

SEN, A.,
  Poverty and Famine - An Essay on Entitlement and Deprivation, Clarendon
  Press, Oxford, 1981.

SIMMONS, A.B.,
  "A Review and Evaluation of Attempts to Constrain Migration to Selected
  Urban Centres and Regions", in UN Population Distribution Policies in
  Development Planning, Population Studies Series N° 75, New York, 1981.

SINGER, H.,
  Technologies for Basic Needs, ILO, Geneva, 1977.

SISLER, D.G., BLANDFORD, D.,
  "Rubber or Rice? -- The Dilemma of Many Developing Nations", World Food
  Issues Series, Centre for the Analysis of World Food Issues, Cornell
  University, Ithaca, 1979.

SOTH, L.,
  "The Grain Export Boom: Should it be Tamed?", in Foreign Affairs,
  Spring 1981.

SPITTLER, G.,
  "The Transition from Subsistence Production to Market-Oriented
  Production Among the Haussa", in Vierteljahresberichte, N° 79, 1980.

SPITZ, P.,
  "Systèmes alimentaires et indépendance nationale", Seminar on the
  Evolution of Algerian Food Consumption, Centre de Recherche en Economie
  Appliquée, Algiers, June 1981.

SPOSITO, E., MEDINA, M.,
  "La réduction de la dépendance agro-alimentaire -- cas du Vénézuela",
  in Cahiers du CENECA, Agriculture et Alimentation, International
  Colloquium, Paris, March 1981.

STATISTISCHES BUNDESAMT,
  Feldstudie Aegypten, Vol. 5, Wiesbaden, 1976.

STEVENS, C.,
     Food Aid and the Developing World - Four African Case Studies,
     London, 1979.

SWEENY, J.,
     "Agriculture Stagnates as Pledged Reforms Remain Unfulfilled", in In-
     ternational Herald Tribune, Special Supplement on Venezuela, May 1980.

TANDON, Y.,
     "New Food Strategies and Social Transformation in East Africa", in
     Africa Development, CODESRIA, Vol. 6, N° 2, 1981.

TARRANT, J.R.,
     "The Geography of Food Aid", in Transactions, Institute of British Geo-
     graphers, Vol. 5, N° 2, 1980.

TATON, R.,
     "Agro-industries alimentaires et cultures vivrières", in Europe Outre-
     mer, N° 610, November 1980.

TIMMER, C.P.,
     "Food Prices and Food Policy Analysis in LDCs", in Food Policy, Vol. 5,
     N° 3, 1980.

TIMMER, C.P., ALDERMAN, H.,
     "Estimating Consumption Parameters for Food Policy Analysis", in
     American Journal of Agricultural Economics, Vol. 61, N° 5, December
     1979.

TOLLEY, G.S., et al.,
     Agricultural Price Policies and the Developing Countries, Johns Hopkins
     University Press, 1982.

TUBIANA, L.,
     "l'Egypte: Agriculture, alimentation et géopolitiques des échanges",
     in Maghreb Machrek, N° 91, 1981.

TUOMI, H.,
     "Food Imports and Neo-Colonialism", in HARLE, V. (Ed.), The Political
     Economy of Food, Saxon House, Farnborough, 1978.

TYLER, P.S.,
     "Misconception of Food Losses", in Food and Nutrition Bulletin, Vol. 4,
     N° 2, April 1982.

UNIDO, "The Importance of Pesticides in Developing Countries", in Industrial
     Production and Formulation of Pesticides in Developing Countries,
     Vol. 1. General Principles and Formulation of Pesticides, 1972.

UNIDO, "First Global Study on the Food Processing Industry", ID/WG-345/3,
     August 1981.

UNITED NATIONS, UN Demographic Yearbook, Special Issue -- Historical
     Supplement, Monthly Bulletin of Statistics, August 1981.

UNITED NATIONS, "Patterns of Urban and Rural Population Growth", Population Studies Series N° 68, New York, 1980.

UNITED NATIONS/ECOSOC, "Concise Report on Monitoring of Population Policies", Population Commission, 20th Session, E/CN.9/338, 1978.

UNITED STATES ACADEMY OF SCIENCES, Genetic Vulnerability of Major Crops, 1972.

UNITED STATES DEPARTMENT OF AGRICULTURE, Food for Peace, 1978 Annual Report, Washington, D.C., 1979.

VERGOPOULOS, K.,
"L'Agriculture périphérique dans le nouvel ordre international -- réflexions sur la question des systèmes alimentaires nationaux", in Revue Tiers Monde, Vol. 12, N° 85, 1981.

WAGSTAFF, H.,
"Food Imports of Developing Countries", in Food Policy, Vol. 7, N° 1, February 1982.

WALLACE, T.,
"The Challenge of Food: Nigeria's Approach to Agriculture 1975-1980", in Canadian Journal of African Studies, Vol. 15, N° 2, 1981.

WALLENSTEEN, P.,
"Scarce Goods as Political Weapons: The Case of Food", in HARLE, V. (Ed.), The Political Economy of Food, Saxon House, Farnborough, 1978.

WEBER, A.,
"The Various Concepts of Self-Sufficiency and International Trade", in Quarterly Journal of International Agriculture, Vol. 20, N° 3, 1981.

WILLIAMS, D., YOUNG, R.,
"La sécurité alimentaire -- moisson des années 1980", Essai Nord-Sud N° 3, Institut Nord-Sud, Ottawa, 1981.

WORLD BANK,
Accelerated Development in Sub-Saharan Africa, Washington, D.C., 1981.

WORLD BANK,
World Development Report, Washington, D.C., 1980, 1981.

WORLD FOOD COUNCIL,
"Report of the Council to the General Assembly", WFC/1981/17, 31st May 1981.

WORLD FOOD COUNCIL,
"Toward a World Without Hunger: Progress and Prospects for Completing the Unfinished Agenda of the World Food Conference", Report by the Executive Director, WFC/1979/3.

OECD SALES AGENTS
DÉPOSITAIRES DES PUBLICATIONS DE L'OCDE

ARGENTINA – ARGENTINE
Carlos Hirsch S.R.L., Florida 165, 4° Piso (Galería Guemes)
1333 BUENOS AIRES, Tel. 33.1787.2391 y 30.7122

AUSTRALIA – AUSTRALIE
Australia and New Zealand Book Company Pty, Ltd.,
10 Aquatic Drive, Frenchs Forest, N.S.W. 2086
P.O. Box 459, BROOKVALE, N.S.W. 2100. Tel. (02) 452.44.11

AUSTRIA – AUTRICHE
OECD Publications and Information Center
4 Simrockstrasse 5300 Bonn (Germany). Tel. (0228) 21.60.45
Local Agent/Agent local :
Gerold and Co., Graben 31, WIEN 1. Tel. 52.22.35

BELGIUM – BELGIQUE
Jean De Lannoy, Service Publications OCDE
avenue du Roi 202, B-1060 BRUXELLES. Tel. 02/538.51.69

BRAZIL – BRÉSIL
Mestre Jou S.A., Rua Guaipa 518,
Caixa Postal 24090, 05089 SAO PAULO 10. Tel. 261.1920
Rua Senador Dantas 19 s/205-6, RIO DE JANEIRO GB.
Tel. 232.07.32

CANADA
Renouf Publishing Company Limited,
61 Sparks Street (Mall), OTTAWA, Ont. KIP 5A6
Tel. (613)238.8985-6
Toll Free: 1-800.267.4164
2182 ouest, rue Ste-Catherine,
MONTRÉAL, Qué. H3H 1M7. Tel. (514)937.3519

DENMARK – DANEMARK
Munksgaard Export and Subscription Service
35, Nørre Søgade
DK 1370 KØBENHAVN K. Tel. +45.1.12.85.70

FINLAND – FINLANDE
Akateeminen Kirjakauppa
Keskuskatu 1, 00100 HELSINKI 10. Tel. 65.11.22

FRANCE
Bureau des Publications de l'OCDE,
2 rue André-Pascal, 75775 PARIS CEDEX 16. Tel. (1) 524.81.67
Principal correspondant :
13602 AIX-EN-PROVENCE : Librairie de l'Université.
Tel. 26.18.08

GERMANY – ALLEMAGNE
OECD Publications and Information Center
4 Simrockstrasse 5300 BONN Tel. (0228) 21.60.45

GREECE – GRÈCE
Librairie Kauffmann, 28 rue du Stade,
ATHÈNES 132. Tel. 322.21.60

HONG-KONG
Government Information Services,
Publications/Sales Section, Baskerville House,
2nd Floor, 22 Ice House Street

ICELAND – ISLANDE
Snaebjörn Jönsson and Co., h.f.,
Hafnarstraeti 4 and 9, P.O.B. 1131, REYKJAVIK.
Tel. 13133/14281/11936

INDIA – INDE
Oxford Book and Stationery Co. :
NEW DELHI-1, Scindia House. Tel. 45896
CALCUTTA 700016, 17 Park Street. Tel. 240832

INDONESIA – INDONÉSIE
PDIN-LIPI, P.O. Box 3065/JKT., JAKARTA, Tel. 583467

IRELAND – IRLANDE
TDC Publishers – Library Suppliers
12 North Frederick Street, DUBLIN 1 Tel. 744835-749677

ITALY – ITALIE
Libreria Commissionaria Sansoni :
Via Lamarmora 45, 50121 FIRENZE. Tel. 579751/584468
Via Bartolini 29, 20155 MILANO. Tel. 365083
Sub-depositari :
Ugo Tassi
Via A. Farnese 28, 00192 ROMA. Tel. 310590
Editrice e Libreria Herder,
Piazza Montecitorio 120, 00186 ROMA. Tel. 6794628
Costantino Ercolano, Via Generale Orsini 46, 80132 NAPOLI. Tel. 405210
Libreria Hoepli, Via Hoepli 5, 20121 MILANO. Tel. 865446
Libreria Scientifica, Dott. Lucio de Biasio "Aeiou"
Via Meravigli 16, 20123 MILANO Tel. 807679
Libreria Zanichelli
Piazza Galvani 1/A, 40124 Bologna Tel. 237389
Libreria Lattes, Via Garibaldi 3, 10122 TORINO. Tel. 519274
La diffusione delle edizioni OCSE è inoltre assicurata dalle migliori librerie nelle
città più importanti.

JAPAN – JAPON
OECD Publications and Information Center,
Landic Akasaka Bldg., 2-3-4 Akasaka,
Minato-ku, TOKYO 107 Tel. 586.2016

KOREA – CORÉE
Pan Korea Book Corporation,
P.O. Box n° 101 Kwangwhamun, SÉOUL. Tel. 72.7369

LEBANON – LIBAN
Documenta Scientifica/Redico,
Edison Building, Bliss Street, P.O. Box 5641, BEIRUT.
Tel. 354429 – 344425

MALAYSIA – MALAISIE
University of Malaya Co-operative Bookshop Ltd.
P.O. Box 1127, Jalan Pantai Baru
KUALA LUMPUR. Tel. 51425, 54058, 54361

THE NETHERLANDS – PAYS-BAS
Staatsuitgeverij, Verzendboekhandel,
Chr. Plantijnstraat 1 Postbus 20014
2500 EA S-GRAVENHAGE. Tel. nr. 070.789911
Voor bestellingen: Tel. 070.789208

NEW ZEALAND – NOUVELLE-ZÉLANDE
Publications Section,
Government Printing Office Bookshops:
AUCKLAND: Retail Bookshop: 25 Rutland Street,
Mail Orders: 85 Beach Road, Private Bag C.P.O.
HAMILTON: Retail: Ward Street,
Mail Orders, P.O. Box 857
WELLINGTON: Retail: Mulgrave Street (Head Office),
Cubacade World Trade Centre
Mail Orders: Private Bag
CHRISTCHURCH: Retail: 159 Hereford Street,
Mail Orders: Private Bag
DUNEDIN: Retail: Princes Street
Mail Order: P.O. Box 1104

NORWAY – NORVÈGE
J.G. TANUM A/S
P.O. Box 1177 Sentrum OSLO 1. Tel. (02) 80.12.60

PAKISTAN
Mirza Book Agency, 65 Shahrah Quaid-E-Azam, LAHORE 3.
Tel. 66839

PHILIPPINES
National Book Store, Inc.
Library Services Division, P.O. Box 1934, MANILA.
Tel. Nos. 49.43.06 to 09, 40.53.45, 49.45.12

PORTUGAL
Livraria Portugal, Rua do Carmo 70-74,
1117 LISBOA CODEX. Tel. 360582/3

SINGAPORE – SINGAPOUR
Information Publications Pte Ltd,
Pei-Fu Industrial Building,
24 New Industrial Road N° 02-06
SINGAPORE 1953, Tel. 2831786, 2831798

SPAIN – ESPAGNE
Mundi-Prensa Libros, S.A.
Castelló 37, Apartado 1223, MADRID-1. Tel. 275.46.55
Libreria Bosch, Ronda Universidad 11, BARCELONA 7.
Tel. 317.53.08, 317.53.58

SWEDEN – SUÈDE
AB CE Fritzes Kungl Hovbokhandel,
Box 16 356, S 103 27 STH, Regeringsgatan 12,
DS STOCKHOLM. Tel. 08/23.89.00
Subscription Agency/Abonnements:
Wennergren-Williams AB,
Box 13004, S104 25 STOCKHOLM.
Tel. 08/54.12.00

SWITZERLAND – SUISSE
OECD Publications and Information Center
4 Simrockstrasse 5300 BONN (Germany). Tel. (0228) 21.60.45
Local Agents/Agents locaux
Librairie Payot, 6 rue Grenus, 1211 GENÈVE 11. Tel. 022.31.89.50

TAIWAN – FORMOSE
Good Faith Worldwide Int'l Co., Ltd.
9th floor, No. 118, Sec. 2,
Chung Hsiao E. Road
TAIPEI. Tel. 391.7396/391.7397

THAILAND – THAÏLANDE
Suksit Siam Co., Ltd., 1715 Rama IV Rd,
Samyan, BANGKOK 5. Tel. 2511630

TURKEY – TURQUIE
Kültur Yayinlari Is-Türk Ltd. Sti.
Atatürk Bulvari No : 191/Kat. 21
Kavaklidere/ANKARA. Tel. 17 02 66
Dolmabahce Cad. No : 29
BESIKTAS/ISTANBUL. Tel. 60 71 88

UNITED KINGDOM – ROYAUME-UNI
H.M. Stationery Office,
P.O.B. 276, LONDON SW8 5DT.
(postal orders only)
Telephone orders: (01) 622.3316, or
49 High Holborn, LONDON WC1V 6 HB (personal calle.)
Branches at: EDINBURGH, BIRMINGHAM, BRISTOL,
MANCHESTER, BELFAST.

UNITED STATES OF AMERICA – ÉTATS-UNIS
OECD Publications and Information Center, Suite 1207,
1750 Pennsylvania Ave., N.W. WASHINGTON, D.C.20006 – 4582
Tel. (202) 724.1857

VENEZUELA
Libreria del Este, Avda. F. Miranda 52, Edificio Galipan,
CARACAS 106. Tel. 32.23.01/33.26.04/31.58.38

YUGOSLAVIA – YOUGOSLAVIE
Jugoslovenska Knjiga, Knez Mihajlova 2, P.O.B. 36, BEOGRAD.
Tel. 621.992

Les commandes provenant de pays où l'OCDE n'a pas encore désigné de dépositaire peuvent être adressées à :
OCDE, Bureau des Publications, 2, rue André-Pascal, 75775 PARIS CEDEX 16.

Orders and inquiries from countries where sales agents have not yet been appointed may be sent to:
OECD, Publications Office, 2, rue André-Pascal, 75775 PARIS CEDEX 16.

67849-07-1984

OECD PUBLICATIONS, 2, rue André-Pascal, 75775 PARIS CEDEX 16 - No. 42929 1984
PRINTED IN FRANCE
(41 84 03 1) ISBN 92-64-12623-6